RAMBLINGS

of a

PSYCHOLOGIST

The Cases and Clients of Dr. Trattoria

Gerald A. Strag, Ed. D.

RAMBLINGS OF A PSYCHOLOGIST: THE CASES AND CLIENTS OF DR. TRATTORIA

1405 SW 6th Avenue • Ocala, Florida 34471 • Phone 352-622-1825 • Fax 352-622-1875
Website: www.atlantic-pub.com • Email: sales@atlantic-pub.com
SAN Number: 268-1250

Library of Congress Cataloging-in-Publication Data

Names: Strag, Gerald, author.
Title: The ramblings of a psychologist / by Gerald A. Strag.
Description: Ocala, Florida : Atlantic Publishing Group, Inc., [2020] |
Summary: "The Ramblings of a Psychologist is a collection of stories based on personal experience as a practicing psychologist"— Provided by publisher.
Identifiers: LCCN 2019047390 (print) | LCCN 2019047391 (ebook) | ISBN 9781620236383 (paperback) | ISBN 9781620236390 (ebook)
Subjects: LCSH: Strag, Gerald—Anecdotes. | Counseling psychologist and client—Anecdotes. | Counseling psychologists—Anecdotes. | Counseling psychology—Anecdotes.
Classification: LCC BF636.6 .S76 2020 (print) | LCC BF636.6 (ebook) | DDC 158.3—dc23
LC record available at https://lccn.loc.gov/2019047390
LC ebook record available at https://lccn.loc.gov/2019047391

Printed in the United States

PROJECT MANAGER: Katie Cline
INTERIOR LAYOUT AND JACKET DESIGN: Nicole Sturk

Table of Contents

The Ramblings of a Psychologist is a collection of stories based on personal experience as a practicing psychologist. Of course, the stories are fictionalized, both to protect my patients from exploitation and to protect myself from lawyers, who have a proclivity for making their money suing psychologists. The stories are a mixture of mystery, autobiography, and philosophy, not necessarily in that order.

The protagonist, Dr. Trattoria, appears in each of the stories expressing his special brand of humor, personal insight, and drama. He considers himself an investigator akin to Sherlock Holmes, but he is actually more like Chief Inspector Clouseau. His serious side has him solving his patient's conundrums one painful dilemma at a time.

There is no answer to the question "what is wrong with me?" when it depends on formulating an answer to a problem that suits someone else. Our human nature is that we learn right and wrong through the consequences of our own actions.

Perhaps the sentiments contained in the following pages are not yet fashionable enough to win general approval. The longer you think of something as right or wrong, you become habituated to that way of thinking. This raises a formidable problem: the belief that right or wrong is based on custom, not reason. Once the turmoil subsides and you have time to think the issue through, you might come to a different conclusion.

Patients learn this time and again through trial and error. It's sad how often the same mistakes have to be repeated. Psychologists hope that eventually the problems are recognized and owned, that the lessons are grasped and put into practice. Therapists usually understand the diagnostic issues but frequently fail to put their insight into context. They recognize the problem but don't understand how it relates to the patient.

Many therapists take the attitude that their patient's problem is an academic exercise. When the therapist recognizes that this is the real deal, the therapeutic insight is lost. Trattoria is one of the few therapists who fully appreciates the magic of the moment and makes every moment count.

Chapter 1

Right and Wrong

Aftertaking a seat in one of my overstuffed chairs, we formally introduced ourselves. After a few awkward moments of silence, Samuel Clements started the conversation.

"What's wrong with me? I am never content. I'm angry all the time. Even when I'm not sad, the joy in my life is missing. When there are good times, they don't last, and then it's down in the dumps I go, and there I stay," Samuel said rapidly. He paused to take a breath before continuing. "Am I cursed to be this way forever? No one understands me."

"Your problem isn't that unique. It's been diagnosed thousands of times by hundreds of therapists," I responded. "Finding an answer to what's wrong with you doesn't have to be like finding a needle in a haystack. All that's necessary is finding someone you trust. It's not like guessing the winning lottery numbers to a Mega Millions jackpot."

"I don't believe someone has to walk in my shoes to understand my problem, but I don't know if I've got what it takes to solve the puzzle."

Samuel paused here. Between fidgeting with his clothing and avoiding eye contact, it was obvious to me that he was internally struggling with what he wanted to say next.

"Why do you think that?" I prompted.

"Well, I just don't know if I can be honest enough with myself to know what the problem is when I see it," Samuel whispered.

"How badly do you want the problem solved?"

"I don't have a life that's worth living. I constantly think it's easier to end it than to put myself through this."

"Have you been thinking of killing yourself for some time?"

"No, I haven't considered suicide!" Samuel said defensively.

"Your words implied differently."

"Well, that is how I feel at my low points. I'm not suicidal all the time. I suppose I exaggerated my desperation to make a point."

"There is a psychologist by the name of David Augsburger who explained your feelings: 'Since nothing we intend is ever faultless, and nothing we attempt ever without error, and nothing we achieve without some measure of finitude and fallibility we call humanness, we are saved by forgiveness.' That could leave you frustrated and angry if you are expecting something different. Do you think Augsburger was on the right track to explaining your feelings?"

"I don't know. If you equate frustration with anger, I guess. Maybe I'm frustrated with myself more than I'm angry. It seems that possibly I have mixed feelings, and I don't get it straight all the time."

"Now you're talking. No one is in charge of their feelings every second of the day. You said you are angry all the time, and that sounds like hyperbole. You talk as if everything you do is flawed. You can't be dismissive of the things you do and control the boundaries to your self-criticism."

Samuel leaned forward. "Are you saying that regardless of what I do, it will never be good enough? According to you, I'm my own worst enemy."

He slumped back into the scuffed black leather chair. I could almost see the despair taking over him.

"Isn't it the nature of man to learn from his mistakes? Right and wrong are learned through the consequences of our own behavior most of the time. Not everyone makes the connection between what they do and how they feel. You're on the right track. All you have to do is love yourself and accept yourself as fallible."

*   *   *

THIS WAS THE only session I had with Samuel. He made up his mind that one session was all he needed. What he ultimately did to resolve his hostility towards himself remains a mystery. Unfortunately, this type of resolution, if you could call it that, is all too common in my line of work. Psychology frequently leads to a black hole in space. Hopefully, your tolerance for ambiguity includes the ability to handle situations that do not lead to classic resolutions.

Chapter 2

To Be or Not to Be

At around 3:30 a.m., a call to my cell phone shattered my sleep. The sound of the "William Tell Overture" is not my favorite orchestral piece that early in the morning. I catapulted out of bed before it woke up my wife, Sophie.

The voice on the other side said, "I need to talk to Dr. Trattoria about an urgent matter."

Bleary-eyed and half out of breath, I responded, "Who is this?"

"My name is Mark. I am not a patient of yours, but I desperately need your help."

"What's causing your dilemma at 3:30 in the morning?" I asked. My regular protocols were kicking in, despite the early hour.

"My life is caving in on me. I'm desperate to find answers to questions I hope you can provide. My problem is with my wife, Sheila. I thought we were a happily married couple, but she started telling me she wants a divorce." His voice became strained. "When I asked her to explain the texts on her phone, all she said was that she wants a divorce. I don't get it, Doc!"

"Perhaps if you could explain to me what the texts said, I might be able to provide some insights for you," I calmly suggested while walking to my home office. This was shaping up to be an intense wake-up call, and I didn't want to wake up Sophie.

"Earlier today, I picked up Sheila's cell phone and read her text messages. Her sexting left nothing to the imagination. When I tried to discuss the affair with her, all she would say was, 'I don't want to talk about it. You're too mad to discuss it.' Over and over again, Sheila kept repeating the same message that she wanted a divorce and child support!"

"How mad does that make you Mark?"

"Furious. Mad enough to shoot the bitch and her two kids and stuff them into large plastic bags and drag them out to the Gulf Stream to feed the sharks."

His rage was palpable. The distance created by the phone lines did little to soften his rage. My eyes were wide open, and the sluggish need for sleep was gone. His threat to kill his family was like a shot of adrenaline.

"I don't have a dog in this fight but that sounds pretty angry. You seem incapable of cloaking your anger, even while talking to me. You have to let your anger out and to trust someone. Venting your pain and anger is the beginning of the healing process."

"How do I vent my anger without acting on my feelings?"

"Your feelings don't cause you to act unless you're wired that way. You planned out everything very carefully. I don't see you as an impulse-driven guy. Am I wrong?"

"No. Most of the time I can manage my life without going off the deep end. But this isn't an everyday event. Sheila has me questioning everything about myself."

I hoped that the children he mentioned had a special place in his heart, despite his initial anger. "What is in the best interest of the children?"

"I don't care what's in their best interest. I'm trying to survive the shock of what she has done to me. Nothing else matters."

"Sheila's behavior seems to have set off an avalanche of anger that threatens to bury your family."

"Can you believe Sheila has the balls to tell me that she wants $1,200 a month for child support and that I need to get the hell out of the house!" Mark whined, seeming to ignore my attempts to direct the conversation.

"Well, what alternative would you suggest? Live in the house with her?"

"Don't be absurd," Mark said with a scoff. "Why would you suggest such a thing? The house belonged to my mother, who gifted it to me in an inheritance eight years ago. I spent most of our savings and all of my extra cash fixing the house to please her. Now that things have gotten rough, and I am short on cash, she plans on throwing me out. She's an evil bitch."

"Okay, say her betrayal is real. Why do you plan on killing the kids? Aren't they innocent in this situation?"

"I adopted Ann and Robbie believing that we were a family. What do you think her 7-year-old daughter and 9-year-old son call me when I tell them to do homework or finish their chores? An asshole!

"Sheila thinks it's funny when the kids call me an asshole in front of my family and our friends," Mark said as he continued to cry and scream into the phone. "It's all too much. I have to kill 'em all."

His voice stopped abruptly.

"How do you plan on killing the kids?" I asked him.

"That's not difficult. One long rifle and a .22 mm bullet an inch above their right eyebrow. That's how I kill my pigs when we have a pig picking," he answered.

"Don't you think that you'll have a more difficult time shooting your kids than you had shooting the pigs?"

"They hurt my feelings day after day. They never stopped their tormenting."

"But they're kids! How will you live with yourself knowing you killed two innocent kids?"

"I don't believe they're so innocent. They kept her secrets for months, laughing at me with her behind my back. That's all the incentive I need to shoot the bitch and her brood."

"Just what will you accomplish by killing the kids?"

"Nothing but the knowledge that they didn't get away with it."

"You're guaranteeing a place for yourself on death row! Are you ready for that?"

My shocking question stopped Mark in his tracks. Not knowing what to say, he kept quiet and recovered his breath. The wounds inflicted by his wife's betrayal seemed insurmountable to him in that moment.

I listened to Mark focus on his pain. The conflict Mark felt about having to kill them all was taking its toll on him emotionally.

"If the state doesn't kill you, how will you feel spending the rest of your life locked up?" I prompted, hoping to dissuade his plan to kill his family.

"I don't know. I think it is justified right now."

"How will your folks handle you killing the kids?"

"They know how my family bullied and humiliated me for years, so it won't be a complete shock that I struck back. They had it coming."

"Really!" I interjected. "They had it coming? You sentence the kids to die for calling you names. Death is the sentence you impose when a 7-year-old calls you an asshole?"

"You're minimizing what they have been doing to me for years. Sheila's whoring around has nothing to do with how I have been made to feel. It's all existential crap as far as you are concerned. Nothing matters to anybody, I guess. I don't know why I'm wasting my time talking to you."

"You're not wasting your time. You need to talk to someone who can be objective. You called me, remember?"

My relationship with Mark was obviously strained at this point. He stopped believing I could help him.

"You're just a bleeding-heart liberal," he said.

"My political opinions have nothing to do with this. This is not just a matter of right and wrong; it's a matter of life and death! The kids are disrespectful, and this drives you crazy. That's a matter for you and your wife to settle. What's wrong with a good ass-whipping?" I asked.

"Nothing is wrong with a whipping," Mark declared. "I suggested giving them a good ass-whipping for years. Sheila won't hear of it. She thinks that's child abuse."

"When the two of you fight, they're going to presume she is right, regardless of what she says or does, because she's their mother. Do you think you become so angry because you're not allowed to settle the problem your own way?" I asked.

"You're God damn right I am! What's wrong with you? Right is right, and wrong is wrong. There is no in between. When she is wrong, she never admits it. I have to take it in stride, and she gets away with it. You've heard an eye for an eye, and a tooth for a tooth? That's all I 'm asking for."

"Was Jesus right when he said, 'Give unto others as you would have them give unto you?'" I quoted.

Mark didn't respond.

I couldn't help but wonder what kind of person I was dealing with. Mark has to be character disordered.

"Wouldn't it be better to end the marriage and rid yourself of all the problems the simple way? It beats ending end up in jail or on death row," I said to him again.

"It's not that simple, I love her and thought that things would get better. For a while they were. That's when we would come together as a family. Maybe Sheila gave up screwing my friends for a little while, but when she got back into her routine of screwing my friends, all hell would break loose!"

With this realization, I began to understand why Mark was so angry. He wasn't dealing only with the betrayal of his wife and the loss of his family, but the betrayal of his friends as well.

"I can't tell if your more upset by your friends or the infidelity of your wife. You thought you could trust your friends, and you took it for granted that you could trust your wife. Maybe you need to question your choice of friends and not take your wife for granted," I gently remarked. "And if you still think that this marriage is over, perhaps focus on getting an attorney and kicking her and the kids to the curb."

I hoped that providing Mark with a viable option that removed Sheila and the kids from his life would save their lives — and his.

"Maybe you're right," Mark said sounding dejected. "I was expecting more from you besides, throw the bitch out. I thought you could make a difference."

"Are you ready to forgive her and your friends? That's what it's going to take to make a difference. I am just providing you with short-term solutions to your problem at the moment, but forgiveness is what you need to focus on for long-term healing and growth."

"I know you're right. How much time is it going to take to get this out of my mind?"

"Years," I told him. "How much do you love her? Are you willing to wear out the thoughts of her fucking your friends?"

"There were a lot of good times, and I wanted to believe that they would last. I thought I could forgive her, but I can't get her fucking around out of my mind. I don't get it, Doc. She's fucking the three stooges, and she wants the divorce.

"She's claiming that she wants a divorce because I read her pornographic phone messages! What am I missing that would help me make sense of this opera?" Mark pleaded with me. "It's okay for her to commit adultery, but I'm slime for reading about her infidelity on her cell phone?"

"Love is complicated. If you love her, then you love her. Love isn't a switch you throw off like a circuit breaker. It doesn't matter what you read in the text messages. It will take time to fall out of love with her," I responded.

Marks anger deflated momentarily, and the raw painful truth made its way to the surface. "I don't have any reason to go on. I just want to die."

"How long have you been thinking of killing yourself?" I asked him again.

"A while I guess," he said. "It's the money, the job, my so-called friends, and all of the rest. I'm going to write a new logo for my T-shirt that says, 'Life Sucks.'"

"Maybe it's time to make a list of the people who love you. You're going to make them casualties too."

"My mother and father. That's it. No one else would miss me. Sheila and the kids would be glad to have me gone. My friends could continue fucking Sheila without worrying about me. It would be for the best that I just end it," Mark said. "I just don't know what is right or wrong, Doc. I need your help sorting through it. How am I going to sort this mess out?"

"One of the oldest methods used to help begins with you writing out your history. This forces you to process who you are and where you are going. Remembering isn't an easy task when it involves others. Your honesty is critical. Remembering who we are means fighting the temptation of making up how you want to be remembered, especially when there is no one to verify the facts."

"I just don't know if I have enough patience for all that, Doc." Mark's speech became labored, as if someone punched him in the gut, and he couldn't get enough air. "It's decision time. I got the bags and the gun. The boat is gassed, and I'm ready for one last trip to the Gulf Stream."

I felt a sudden chill and knew I had to think fast or lose the client and his family.

"Can we talk about it and see if there is any option besides killing them all? Do you want to meet me at the hospital to talk about alternatives? I can be there in 20 minutes."

"No, Doc, I can't do that. The minute I show up at the hospital, you'll have cops wrestle me to the ground and cuff me. That sounds like a lose/lose proposition to me," Mark said.

"The hospital is a safe public place, and no one will get hurt," I pleaded.

"Safe for whom, me or you?" Mark said. "The cops are all carrying guns."

"I'm the only one who won't be packing," I responded. "We don't have a track record and neither of us knows if the other can be trusted. How do you feel about meeting me at my office?"

"How's that any different?" he asked. "What guarantee do I have that cops won't be at your office."

"So far you haven't killed any of your family? Am I right?"

"That's right!" Mark screamed. "But if you keep up your shit, you might be the first one I shoot."

If this sudden change in mood — and threat on my life — was intended to frighten me, it had the opposite effect. It only hardened my resolve to help him. Mark seemed to have lost the score card of who is on his side. His grip on reality was slipping.

"You haven't committed a crime," I reminded him. "Thinking about killing someone is not the same as committing murder. You can't be arrested for fantasies of killing someone. Maybe we can work out a solution to the problems with Sheila, and you won't go to prison or lose your family.

"Will I be arrested?" Mark asked.

"As I told you earlier, you have not committed a crime, and you won't be arrested. However, I'm legally required to inform the police that threats have been made against your family and yourself. If your wife and kids are safe, you are home free. You can have a life and you can live any way that you want."

When Mark didn't respond, I began to feel as if I hadn't made a connection with the man on the phone.

"Come to my clinic, and let's see if we can work it out. I'm getting more and more confused talking to you on the phone. You say that you want help because you don't want to kill your family. It is obvious that you have given a lot of thought to killing them. When I offer you the option of working it out without killing them, you threaten to kill me. Your love and hate issues are scary."

"If you think you're frightened, you ought to be standing in my boots," he said.

"How can I advise you about anything when I don't know what you want or what you are capable of doing?" I asked. "Why don't you come to my office, and we can talk through all of your issues and try to find a satisfactory solution."

"Fine," Mark reluctantly agreed. "But I'd better not be ambushed once I get there."

"I wouldn't violate your trust like that," I reassured him. "Now do you know how to get to my office?"

"No, but I have a GPS. I will be at the office soon," Mark said before hanging up the phone.

*   *   *

THE FADED LETTERS embossed on the modest hand carved sign read "Dr. Anthony Trattoria, Ph.D. Psychologist." It is the first thing anyone sees when they enter the parking lot. As I looked around from my Miata, I discovered that I was the only one there. Before I left home to meet Mark, I called the police for assistance. A police dispatcher answered the call.

"This is Judith Whitley. You have reached the Jacksonville Police Department. What is your emergency?"

"This is Dr. Trattoria, and I am calling about a homicidal patient."

"Can you verify who you are by giving me your address and phone number? Please give me your cell phone number first in case we get disconnected. I will get the sergeant on the line," Dispatcher Whitley said and placed me on hold.

Tic, toc, tic toc. Time passed slowly, like an old pendulum clock, as I waited for someone to respond. Suddenly there was a baritone voice on the phone. "This is Sergeant Flowers. What is the emergency, Doctor Trattoria?"

"I have a patient who called me at about 3:30 this morning threatening to kill his family. He goes by the name of Mark, but he didn't give me a last name."

"How do you know he has not killed them?"

"I don't know for sure that he has not acted on his impulse, but he claimed they were still alive."

"Do you know this man?" Sergeant Flowers asked.

"No, I have no recollection of him. I'll have to wait till I get on my computer and access my files to make sure, however."

"How soon will you be able to do that?" Sergeant Flowers asked.

"As soon as I make it to my office in about 15 minutes. I will call you if I locate a file on him. When I tried to set up a meeting with him at the ER, he refused the meeting. He said he didn't feel it was safe."

"Do you think he's had a run in with the police before?" Sergeant Flowers asked.

"Anything is possible. Later in the conversation he agreed to meet me at my office, which doesn't make sense! Why would he be any safer in my office than at the hospital?"

"Could it be that something has happened at the hospital before, like a commitment or something equally traumatic?"

"You're asking important questions that I have no way of answering. Maybe he doesn't want his picture taken. There are security cameras all over the lobby," I suggested.

"It could be that the victim is someone yet to be discovered, and he doesn't want to let the cat out of the bag. Have you considered the risk this puts you in, Doctor?" asked Sergeant Flowers. "Do you know if he's armed?"

I cleared my throat. "I don't believe that I am at risk of getting shot. His family is another issue entirely. They're in harm's way. The risk I take comes with the job. We both know that. I've got to get a bigger life insurance policy!" I said, and we both laughed.

"I don't mean to raise your blood pressure or make your job more stressful, but do you own a gun?" Sergeant Flowers asked.

"Yes, I do own several guns, but I routinely leave my guns at home. I'm making my way to the office as we speak," I responded. "I told him I was legally required to inform the police about the threats, and he took the news in stride."

"Okay, I will send two police cruisers to the office with members of our SWAT team," Sergeant Flowers informed me.

"There won't be blaring sirens and blue flashing lights, right?" I asked. "Flashing lights and sirens are a formula for driving people over the top."

"My agenda is to keep everyone alive while respecting their rights. I'm reminded of individual rights every day. I give each joker his rights in the Miranda warning at least once day."

"You know, I don't think the Founding Fathers stopped to consider the man who threatens to kill his family with a gun when they wrote the First and Second Amendments. When they wrote about the right to free speech and the right to bear arms, they were writing about armed insurrection and fighting the British."

"I'm familiar with the Constitution, but it doesn't change my responsibility. The law is the law, and the nuts have rights too," Sergeant Flowers said.

"Alright, we can argue about this over a cup of coffee sometime soon. For now, we should focus on the case. I do have one question about protocol. How can you get information from me if I will be in my office and the officers will be sitting in police cruisers in the parking lot?"

"Leave your cell phone on after he arrives. If we discover that the man is dangerous and/or has committed a crime, we will move in to secure him and take him into custody. Do you have any more questions?"

"No, none that come to mind. I'll have to play it by ear," I responded. In reality, I was suffering from Blue Collar syndrome; my mind was full of questions, none of which I asked. I didn't know what questions needed to be asked and which questions could be ignored. "I just want your assurance that your team won't come in with guns blazing. If I feel that I am in danger, I'll let you know."

My anxiety was getting worse as I got closer to my office. My stomach was tying itself in knots. I could feel cold sweat running down my face and the back of my neck. I wasn't sure if I was going to soil myself or throw up — or both.

I just tried to remind myself that the drama that started this morning has an end time. Things will go back to normal.

Sergeant Flowers's voice cut off my reverie. "As soon as I can verify his wife and children are safe, we will let you know." Let's end this conversation on a positive note. With a little luck, we will have coffee and donuts within the hour."

*   *   *

AS I WALKED to the front door of my office, I was struck by my vulnerability and the danger I was about to confront. This morning's crisis call was frightening, like being home alone in the middle of the night and suddenly seeing a stranger looking at you through the curtain of your bedroom window. Getting a call from a stranger who is threatening to kill his wife and children would get anyone's pulse racing.

The beast who made the call said his name was Mark. That didn't mean a thing; who the hell is Mark? Who have I seen in the last five years who might be capable of doing something like this?

Walking into the office, I stumbled on yesterday's mail. Taking a knee, I picked up the bills, insurance envelopes, and junk mail lying on the floor and walked to my office.

This office isn't home, but it's where I have spent more than half of my life. For 27 years, I have occupied the same office suite with only minor additions: a table here, a new lamp there.

The waiting room is bright with sunshine coming in from a door window and a standard 56-inch window at the other end of the room. There are no Queen Anne chairs to give the room a look of sophistication, but instead functional steel framed chairs covered with black artificial leather seats and backs line the walls.

The feeling the waiting room communicates is that something serious is going to happen, and there is no time for nonsense.

I still hadn't had any luck identifying him from recent memory. I turned on my computer and begin to search my archives for Mark. *No luck*, I said to myself. *I haven't a clue who you are, Mark. You are the phantom of my opera.*

I couldn't help but wonder what Mark's real objection to meeting at the hospital emergency room was. Perhaps it was just the cameras, as Sergeant Flowers thought, but his sarcasm on the phone caught me off guard. It suggested that the man on the phone might have a different agenda.

Who is this guy, and who does he really want to kill?

If the call from Mark was a legitimate crisis, then there was a chance that I would be able to resolve the problem without bloodshed. But if the caller had a more sinister intention, there was the possibility that I would never see my wife again.

I had to get my mind out of these dark thoughts. I thought perhaps Sophie would have an idea of who Mark was — she could always navigate my records better than I could — and decided to give her a call.

"Good morning, Sophie. I know it's early, and I hate to wake you, but would you be able to help me out?"

"Are you ok?" Sophie asked, the concern evident in her voice.

"Yes, I'm ok," I reassured her. "I had an emergency with a homicidal client and had to get to the office. I can't go into detail right now, but I'm not hurt."

"What do you need?" Sophie asked.

"Will you draw up a list of patients who I committed in the last six months. The list of patients might be a good starting point to help me sort out who the monster is."

"Whoever it is, he must be a few cards short of a full deck. He's obviously not a rational man," Sophie said. "Do you think he is suicidal?"

"That could make sense. Suppose he plans on dying, then he doesn't have anything to lose by letting the world know who he is. I guess he may want someone to know the history of events." If this is the case, my diagnosis was probably wrong; he is probably not a psychopath, just a guy trying to even a score.

"And that someone had to be you?" Sophie asked.

"I don't think there was a motive behind calling me. I just happened to be the first search result that turned up," I said. "But go and see if you can find any record of him, and please be quick. The way he's going on about murdering his family suggests that he's not planning to get away with it alive."

I guess Sophie could have been right. Maybe death by suicide was his intension all along. Maybe he was hoping that the cops would kill him if he threatened one of them.

While I waited for an update from Sophie and for Mark to show up, I started organizing my office to keep busy and my mind off of the worst-case scenarios. It was a little creepy to be at the office this early. The streets outside were quiet, and no one was around.

As I was setting the mail on my receptionist's desk, I was startled by the office phone ringing and dropped it all. I darted to the phone. "Hello!" I shouted as it went dead. With no caller ID, there was no way for me to know who called.

Shit! Calm down old man, I thought and tried to comfort myself by running my hand through my hair. Almost without thinking, I used my cell phone to call Sophie, who picked up on the first ring.

"Hi, babe. Did you just call the office?"

"Yes, I went through your files here at home, and I don't see anything related to a Mark. I'm really worried about you at the office alone. This man sounds dangerous."

"It's okay. I called the police, and they are on their way to the office as we speak. Don't worry, I'll call you after the client leaves and will tell you all of the details," I said, trying to reassure her.

"What took so long for you to get to the phone?" she asked.

"I was down on my knees picking up some clutter and thought while I was down there, I might as well say my prayers," I joked, trying to lighten the mood and ease Sophie's concerns.

Sophie laughed and was grateful that at least her husband hadn't lost his sense of humor. "Do you want me to come to the office? I can bring you coffee and pick up a couple of donuts. I can be there in 20 minutes."

"No! That isn't necessary. Things are under control. I'll be home soon; just get comfortable and don't worry."

"Alright. Let the police handle this. I'm too young to be a widow. Love you," Sophie said and hung up.

* * *

WHO DOES HE think he's fooling? Sophie wondered. She recognized the stress in her husband's voice and knew that he was just trying to ease her worry; things really weren't all under control.

Sophie's tension became too much for her to handle. She decided to get dressed and go to the office.

* * *

ABOUT 20 MINUTES after I hung up with Sophie, I saw a set of headlights coming through the office window toward the front of the building. I immediately called 9-1-1, thinking it must be Mark at last.

Dispatcher Whitley answered the call. "This is the Jacksonville Police Department. What is your emergency?"

"This is Dr. Trattoria; I need to talk to Sergeant Flowers."

"He is not in the office, Dr. Trattoria," Dispatcher Whitley said. "Please hold, and I will patch you through to his cell phone."

About a minute later, I heard Sergeant Flowers' voice on the line. "Any calls from Mark since we last talked?"

"No, but I see headlights outside of my office. I think it might be him," I said, trying to keep my voice steady.

"Okay, stay on the line with me. Just stay calm and use your head."

In the silence, I heard a car door close. A few seconds later, the office door was breached.

"Hello?" I called out. "Mark, is that you?"

"It's me!" Sophie shouted. "I got here as quickly as I could."

I breathed out a sigh. Once again, Sophie proved that she was an unsinkable Molly Brown character.

I held the phone back to my face. "Sergeant, it's just my wife, not Mark."

"Damn it," Sergeant Flowers responded. "I was hoping we'd put this to an end soon. What do you think is going on with him?"

I let my feelings show. "I'm as much in the dark as you. This has been one of the most trying mornings I've had in a long time. He's a mystery. I have no idea what Mark intends to do or where he is."

"It's possible that he's decided to move ahead with his plans," Sergeant Flowers said.

"I don't know what to tell you, Sergeant. He might have killed all of them, but I don't think so. I got the feeling that he was looking for approval and support. I don't think he can count on his folks or any of his friends for that. He needs me," I said.

"Well, time is running out. I don't see any workable solution to resolving the problem. When the SWAT team arrives, I'll leave one of the cars in the back of the office complex for as long as you feel it is necessary. I meant what I told you earlier: you decide what seems reasonable, and we'll do what we can to help," Sergeant Flowers said.

"Thank you, Sergeant," I said and hung up.

I turned to Sophie. "What are you doing here?" I demanded.

"There is no cause for that tone," Sophie responded.

"I told you I would come home soon."

"You weren't being honest with me about all this. I can tell when you're hiding something."

"I tell you what you need to know, and this was not anything you can help me with."

"You tell me that you are waiting in your office for a nut with a gun and you expect me to stay home?" Sophie yelled, tears in her eyes.

"That's precisely the reason that I told you not to come. Don't you think that I have enough to worry about without adding the girl of my dreams to the problem?"

"I want to know what exactly was said, and don't leave out the details."

I gave her a quick summary of the phone call with Mark.

"You can stay for a little while, but if Mark shows up, you have stay in the file room behind the boxes. I mean it."

"Why should I hide behind the file boxes when you're meeting him face-to-face?"

"That's my job. I don't have any choice. If I don't see him and he kills his family, I could not live with myself."

"Yes, you do have a choice. Let the police take over the case."

"That solution that might work if I knew who he was and where he lived, but I don't know him. I don't know anything about him. All I know is I have to protect his family," I said.

Sophie reluctantly agreed to my terms and made me a cup of coffee.

At 5:30 a.m., two hours after the initial call, I decided that Mark was not going to show. I called Sergeant Flowers to cancel the security detail.

"I'm sorry about the drama. I probably screwed it up when I told him that the police would be at the office, I apologize."

"You've been very professional handling a difficult situation. You have nothing to apologize for. I'd like to send a patrol car to your house to be sure you don't have an unannounced house guest. And if it's okay with you, I'll leave an unmarked car in your neighborhood for the next 24 hours."

"That'll take a load off my mind. There was the possibility that he would switch targets, and that made me nervous. Thank you again, Sergeant."

"Sophie it's time to go home," I called out after hanging up with Sergeant Flowers. Sophie scurried about the office turning off the computers and lights. It was still dark in the parking lot, the hint of day just barely on the horizon. I held the front door open for Sophie and walked her to her car as the police cruiser pulled out from behind the building.

The ride home was uneventful, and the traffic on I-95 was just beginning to pick up as we turned our cars onto Ocean Front Drive. Behind us was the unmarked police cruiser.

Once inside, I asked Sophie, "Coffee, bacon, and eggs or a glass of wine?"

"Is that a rhetorical question or are you trying to be funny?" We roared with laughter. I walked over to the china cabinet and got out one long-stemmed wine glass. I know Sophie's wine preference, so I picked up a bottle of Glenn Ellen Chardonnay. I opened the bottle and poured her a glass. She was busy fixing a pot of coffee and half a loaf of toast for the security detail outside. "No sense letting them go hungry," she said.

Once the coffee and toast were ready, I carried a tray filled with goodies out to the cops.

"If there is anything you need, please let me know. I can't tell you how much we appreciate you standing guard," I said, breathing a deep sigh of relief. "Hopefully the rest of the morning will be as peaceful as it was yesterday." With that, I turned and went back into the house.

Maybe Sophie was right; there has to be an easier way to make a living. Cases like this are tough, but I would be lying if I said I did not love them. No dull moments in the life and career of a psychologist. Sophie doesn't have the need for excitement and fosters no wish to be a hero. Maybe that's a man thing, the need to be a hero once in a while. There isn't any social recognition of being a hero, but that's ok; it's how I see myself. I know that I make a difference in the lives of my patients.

Chapter 3

The Beginning of the End

Tuesday, September 11, 2001 started out as a typical day for the Trattorias. The only things scheduled were work at the office and a consultation at Two Rivers Nursing Home. CNN was on when we saw the breaking news: a plane had just flown into the North Tower of the World Trade Center.

Smoke began billowing out of the windows of the stricken tower and left a gaping hole on the side of the building.

"I can't believe it!" Sophie cried.

"We'll have to stay tuned to CNN to find out what happened. The sky was clear; this wasn't an accident," I said.

Just then, a second plane hit the South Tower.

"This is no accident," I repeated. "We're under attack. Look at the television! There are hundreds, if not thousands, of people being killed."

"Terrorists," Sophie cried. "How can this be? I thought the government was supposed to protect us?"

"They can't be everywhere all the time."

"I want to know how these terrorists got those planes. Do you think they are radical Islamic extremists?" Sophie said.

"I don't know, but I'll bet that al-Qaeda is behind it. They'll have confirmation of this within an hour. They can't wait to tell the world what they did to Americans.

"What a way to start the day!" Sophie said. "Is this real? If this is a dream, it is a nightmare."

*　　*　　*

THE ACTIONS ON September 11, 2001 created a nightmare for the entire country, a nightmare that many would never wake up from. The terrorists flew the hijacked plane, American Airlines Flight 11, into the North Wall of the World Trade Center at 8:46 a.m. The plane was flying at 530 mph when it crashed into the North Tower.

After the attack, the United States went to war. The War on Terror primarily took place in Afghanistan, where members of al-Qaeda were headquartered and sheltered by the Taliban government. In 2002, we invaded Iraq after claims were made of weapons of mass destruction.

The terrorist attack on 9/11 and the subsequent wars led to increased occurrences of mental issues, primarily Post-Traumatic Stress Disorder (PTSD) in returning soldiers and survivors of 9/11.

*　　*　　*

ONE MORNING A few months after September 11, Sophie and I were having a quiet breakfast at home when the phone rang. It was the office of personnel management from the Marine Air Station at Cherry Point.

"Good Morning, Doc. This is Sergeant Cobb. Do you have any time to see some men who appear to be suffering from PTSD?"

"Of course, Sergeant."

"The first marine needing your services is Corporal Jeremy Olson. Jeremy has a history of PTSD and a history of addiction. He reports feeling suicidal, and he has started drinking heavily."

"Sergeant, have you hospitalized Mr. Olson as a precaution?"

"There is nowhere to place him other than the barracks. We assigned him a mentor to keep an eye on him. The mentor has worked as a mental health support to men in the past. He is there to protect him from himself, but this can't go on forever."

"Unfortunately, my schedule is pretty full the next few weeks. I'll call the mental health center and find out who is available. If there isn't someone to see them, I'll work them into my schedule somehow."

"Thank you, I appreciate your help."

"I have a few moments before my next appointment comes in. What can you tell me about the men before we meet?"

"Olson just made corporal before he was shipped out to Iraq. He was brought back after his unit incurred steep losses. Two of his friends were not so fortunate; they called themselves The Three Musketeers. They were killed by a roadside bomb on a convoy to western Iraq, along with Terence Barnich, a deputy director of the State Department's Iraq Transition Office in Baghdad. An informant later said that the ambush was intended to kill him. The others were collateral damage.

"Fortunately for Olson, he was walking alongside the Hummer when the bomb was detonated. The explosion was so powerful that the engine was melted down to the tires, and the truck was thrown 15 feet into the air, barely missing Olson. The men sitting in the truck were incinerated.

"Shortly after the ambush, the violence fell off dramatically because the Sunni fighters turned on al-Qaeda and joined U.S forces.

Olson must feel like his friend's deaths were for nothing, that they almost made it out."

"Unfortunately, this is an all-too-common condition that many soldiers have upon their return. We call this survivor's guilt."

"Well, I can understand that feeling, Dr. Trattoria. I've lost many colleagues in my career. Hopefully, you can help Olson, though.

"Lance Corporal Steven O'Malley was a real card. He loved a good time, getting into fights, and writing to his girlfriend. The guys in his unit considered him hen-pecked, although he was not married. O'Malley was the type of guy that never knew a stranger. Everyone who met him, loved him. He came back a victim of the war without a recognizable wound. O'Malley is now seen as reclusive, paranoid, and maybe delusional. He lost all interest in his girlfriend. There has been no mention of suicide, but he's on my radar screen just to be safe.

"Lance Corporal Kenya Smith was just a regular guy. He got along with everybody and kept to himself, never offering an opinion unless he was asked. Most of the men liked him. He never talked badly about his fellow marines. When he was shipped out of the action zone, his persona changed. He went out of his way to antagonize everyone. Smith found hidden meaning in every conversation and was ready to fight at a moment's notice. He became despised by most of the men in his platoon, but a few men were willing to accommodate his need to fight."

* * *

THE SECOND CALL that morning was from a woman named Linda Parnell.

"Dr. Trattoria's office," Sophie said. "How may I help you?"

"My name is Linda Parnell. I called your office to see if Dr. Trattoria is accepting new patients."

"He is. Would you like an appointment? He can see you this afternoon if you're in crisis."

"I'm in crisis, and I need to see him as soon as possible."

"Can you be here at 3 p.m.?"

"That will be great. I'll be there."

*   *   *

LINDA PARNELL SHOWED up right on time for the appointment and was anxious to begin.

"Good afternoon, Mrs. Parnell. I understand you are in a crisis," I said after bringing her back to my office.

"Yes, my problems started after the 9/11 attack on the World Trade Center. I lived in Manhattan at the time of the attack. The dust and debris showered me, and I've been sick ever since. I felt like Chicken Little standing there shouting, 'The sky is falling, the sky is falling.' But that was what it felt like.

"People were all around me pushing and shoving to get away from the dust and debris. There was nowhere to go. All the department stores were packed with people looking to get out of the dust shower. I remember hearing something that sounded like loud claps of thunder, then all at once stuff started to fall. I later learned this was the second tower collapsing. Smoke and debris darkened the sky. People were jumping from the windows to get away from the fire."

"That had to be a terrifying feeling of helplessness to watch," I said.

"I thought the world was coming to an end. It became increasing difficult to breathe, and I started spitting up blood. The dust also caused a rash to develop that covered all of my body. The itching became unbearable, and I scratched myself till I bleed. I tried every remedy that you can buy over the counter, but nothing helped. It's been three weeks since I last had any meaningful sleep. Whenever I do get to sleep, I wake up screaming. I feel like I'm jumping from a window to get away from the flames. Other times, I feel trapped in the building, and I can't get out. I scream, but no one hears me."

"It sounds like you're trying to resolve the trauma by yourself. The feeling of being trapped in the building is representative of you feeling trapped within your trauma. You need someone to guide you through it, much like a firefighter would lead you out of a burning building.

"I'm not a firefighter, but I can help you to get over the trauma. In order to help, I need your cooperation. You're going to have to trust me. We will need at least 10 sessions to give you control of your night terrors. Do you have the patience to work with me going through your nightmares one at a time?" I asked her.

"Yes, of course I do. There's no other rational alternative."

"The first thing we have to do is get you to sleep through the night. If you're ready, we can start now with relaxation therapy."

Linda nodded nervously, indicating that she was ready, if a bit apprehensive."

"Don't worry, Linda." I said. "This practice is just a meditative exercise to help you relax and hopefully sleep. Now let's get started.

"Okay, get comfortable and let yourself slouch and sink in the chair. Let your eyes rest comfortably closed and repeat the word 're-lax' silently to yourself. I'm going to count from 1 to 10. As I get closer to 10, you will find it harder to remember where you are, and you will find yourself more relaxed."

"I feel like you are hypnotizing me," Linda said.

"Relaxation exercises are similar to hypnosis-inducing techniques, but there are no hypnotic suggestions. Are you okay with what I'm suggesting?"

"Okay so far."

"If at any time you find yourself uncomfortable, open your eyes and focus on what is happening to you. You're in complete control; you can't do anything you don't want to do.

"One, take a deep breath and let it out. Relax.

"Two, breath normally. Orient to what is happening.

"Three, relax deeper and deeper. You will find yourself wanting to dream, drifting in and out of sleep.

"Four, five. Relax. Feel your legs and arms and notice how heavy they have become. As you feel more and more relaxed, let your mind support you and know how safe it feels.

"Six, seven. Let go even more. Feel safe and trust your instincts. You are aware of what's going on around you.

"Eight, nine. Sleep deeply. You're in control and relaxed. Stay asleep as long as you want."

I let her rest for a few minutes before gently waking her up.

"Well, how do you feel?" I asked her.

"I feel as if I slept for hours," she said.

"Anytime you want to sleep, you can use this technique. You have it within yourself to do it on your own. The more you practice the technique, the faster you'll fall asleep. When you're ready to resume normal activities, you can suggest to yourself to wake up and feel pleasantly rested, much as you do right now."

"Wow, thank you, Dr. Trattoria. I feel much better than I did when I entered your office. Do you really think we can resolve my issues in just 10 sessions?

"Maybe we can. If not 10 sessions, then may be 12 or 13. Not everyone resolves trauma and heals from traumatic events at the same pace. There are always pre-existing conditions and events in our lives that predispose us one way or the other. This will slow up the process."

*   *   *

A WEEK AFTER my phone call from Sergeant Cobb, he called again.

"Hi, Doc. What have you heard from the mental health center concerning appointments for O'Malley, Olsen, and Smith?"

"Not a thing. I guess I'm your only option."

"When can you see them?"

"How about Thursday this week at 4 p.m.? If it's okay with you, I'd like to do a group session with all three men. As I mentioned, my schedule is a bit tight right now, and this way I can see all three men. They're suffering from similar problems, and a form of group therapy would be beneficial to all of them.

"The more the merrier," said Sergeant Cobb.

"You can bring the three of them to the office for their initial interview. They will be told about EMDR and introduced to relaxation exercises. Assuming everything goes smoothly, I can individualize their treatments during their second visits."

*   *   *

ON THURSDAY AT 4 o'clock, the office looked like a recruiting station for the Marines. All three men arrived wearing combat fatigues and boots, looking for a fight. They filled the waiting room creating a secure presence. Sitting tall and on the edge of their chairs, they looked like statues. They sat quietly. No one was talking as they waited their turn to be seen. This was a new experience. The waiting room became somber as time wound its self-down.

"Good afternoon, gentlemen, I'm Doctor Trattoria. I understand that you are here for treatment of PTSD? This is a provisional diagnosis given to you by your history of combat. Will please you follow me?"

All three men rose to follow me into my office. I could see that their anxiety was starting to skyrocket as they looked around the room nervously.

"Gentlemen, just relax. There isn't a need to protect yourselves from being attacked in here. Take a few moments to introduce yourselves to one another before we get started."

The men mumbled their introductions, and a few minutes later, we were ready to begin the relaxation exercise.

"I am going to introduce you to EMDR. The acronym stands for Eye Movement, Desensitize and Reprogramming. This process was discovered by Dr. Francine Shapiro, a psychologist in California. She developed it on accident following a consultation with her doctor, who gave her a breast cancer diagnosis.

"She became obsessed with the bad news and decided to clear her mind by taking a walk. Fortunately, there was a park nearby in which she could stretch her legs. Francine noticed that the longer she walked, the less anxious she became. She was shifting her attention, and that somehow influenced her thought process. Even when disturbing thoughts came back into her mind, she was less anxious about the news. This was serendipity in its purist form.

"Spontaneously, her eyes began to move rapidly from side to side. The eye movement seemed to cause her thoughts to shift out of consciousness. When she allowed the thoughts to resurface, they did not upset her as much. When she moved her eyes from side to side again, the thoughts faded away, and the anxiety was gone."

O'Malley broke the ice and started off the questions. "What's this all about? We don't have cancer, so how is this going to help us?"

"You don't have to be a cancer patient to benefit from the technique. I told you the story of Dr. Shapiro and how she discovered EMDR to make you aware of how it works.

"I assume all of you are comfortable. If you are not comfortable, try and get comfortable. This isn't a command. Just a suggestion." All three men began to move in their seats, searching for the comfortable spot.

"If at any time you find yourself uncomfortable, open your eyes and focus on what is going on around you. You're in control here, and you can't do anything that you don't want to do."

Once the men appeared to be settled in, I started the session in earnest.

"Let's begin. One, take a deep breath, and let it out. Relax.

"Two, breath normally. Orient to what is happening.

"Three, relax deeper and deeper. You will find yourself wanting to dream, drifting in and out of sleep.

"Four, five. Relax. Feel your legs and arms and notice how heavy they have become. As you feel more and more relaxed, let your mind support you and know how safe it feels.

"Six, seven. Let go. Trust your instincts. You are aware of what's going on around you.

"Eight, nine. Sleep, deeply sleep. You're in control and relaxed. Stay asleep long as you want."

For a few moments, the men were quiet. The only sounds in the room were of them breathing. Within a few minutes, all three men had opened their eyes.

"Welcome back," I said. "Anytime you want to sleep, you can use this technique. When you're ready to resume normal activities, you can suggest to yourself to wake up and feel pleasantly rested."

There was a moment of feeling that we were on our way to successfully resolving their distress. My optimism was short-lived.

"I can't relax. I feel as if I was in someone's AK-47 cross-hairs," O'Malley said.

"It is not unusual to feel anxiety in connection with the event you are trying to resolve. This is called an abreaction. Could you feel each hair on the back of your neck stand at attention?"

"Yes, how did you know?" The sweat was pouring from O'Malley. It looked as if he had been doused by a pitcher of beer. Before I could answer, Smith interrupted.

"I didn't feel relaxed at all. I could hear your instructions, and I did what you asked, but that was it."

"I nearly fell asleep several times," Olson said. "I had to tell myself to stay awake."

"Your varying reactions to the exercise are typical. As we practice the technique, you will get better at recognizing when and where to use it. Your habits are so routine that you don't realize when you are using them. They are skills that you acquired on your own without realizing it."

O'Malley and Smith took six weeks to learn to control their anxiety. The treatment had to be individualized, as each of them had a unique set of traumatic experiences. O'Malley had a duel diagnosis of addiction and PTSD. Smith's problem was borderline personally disorder and PTSD.

Both men had anger issues that would take weeks to resolve. Smith had ego deficits, such as lack of impulse control and poor frustration tolerance. O'Malley had anger related to a history of physical abuse.

Fear of being killed was not the issue related the war in Afghanistan but began a long time ago.

Linda Parnell followed through with the treatment plan. Her sleep disorder was resolved. Fear of dying in the inferno took a little longer to resolve. Other issues of fear of intimacy took months to resolve. The trauma of the relationship with her first husband was insidious. Nothing is as simple as it appears to be.

Chapter 4
The Light at the End of the Tunnel

Bill Anderson called my office with an urgent request to be seen regarding a family matter.

"He can see you on Tuesday afternoon, if that is convenient," Sophie said. "Will you be coming by yourself or with your significant other?"

"I thought it would be better if I came alone first and spelled out the issues from my point of view. I'm sure my wife's thoughts are a lot different from mine, and he'll want to collect her thoughts at some point. I think it would be best if he saw us separately, at first."

"Alright, we will see you on Tuesday."

*   *   *

ON TUESDAY AFTERNOON, Bill showed up for the appointment and spent 15 minutes filling out the intake sheets. Bill is about 6 foot 4 inches tall and walks with long strides. Conservative in appearance, he looked like a man with the weight of the world on his shoulders. He appeared depressed and defeated, and he showed it in his face, with deep circles under his eyes and a sense of listlessness in his movements.

"Hello, Mr. Anderson, what can I do for you this afternoon?" I asked as Bill got settled.

"I'm having a problem with my stepchildren and, subsequently, with my wife."

"How long has this been going on?" I asked.

"Not very long. But then again, I haven't been married very long.

"I suppose I should start from the beginning. Within months of losing my first wife to cancer, I started seeing Barbara, my second wife. I know all about the issues of bereavement, which are far from resolved, but I was lonely and depressed and saw this as a way out of the quagmire.

"My wife-to be was a social worker at Two Rivers Nursing Home. I thought this was serendipitous. I needed a good social worker to talk to, and suddenly, there she was.

"It was love at first sight, and she made a lasting impression. All I could think of throughout the day was her. She was a good listener, and I needed to talk. Her vitality was overwhelming, and her smile and laughter were intoxicating. Her mood was light, and she never exhibited a dark idea. It wasn't something that I was used to having in my life, and this made her exceptionally beautiful.

"We have an age difference of 15 years, which is one of the obstacles we face. For example, when we take a casual stroll, I have a hard time keeping up with her. I can still hear her answer to the question 'Are you going to keep-up this pace?' The answer that I was hoping for was 'no,' but instead she said, 'Yes, but I want to start jogging as soon as you're in good enough shape to do it with me.'

"I feel as though I will never be in enough shape to keep up with her. I feel as if I need a 10-speed bike to keep up with her now. While that example focuses on the physical aspects of our relationship, I'm quite sure it's a metaphor for the rest of our life.

"I frequently try to reassure her, telling her that she's the light at the end of my tunnel, and I'm with her all the way. But I don't know. I feel as if I have more excuses than the average man for the things going wrong in my life. For example, working against our success are Barbara's two teenage girls, Crystal and Leah."

"How do you mean?" I asked.

"The girls had grave reservations about another man intruding on their relationship with their mother. They have the fantasy that Barbara and their father will get back together. Barbara assures me that will never happen. She divorced him because he was narcissist and had no time for her or the girls. Adding to the obstacle is the fact that is he is married to someone else and has been for 10 years."

"Wow, that's quite a rescue fantasy, although it's typical of children of divorce," I said. "I can give you some tools to help gain their trust and love, but I assume that isn't the only problem you're facing in your struggle keeping the family together."

"No, it isn't," Bill said with a deep sigh. "The girls have become accustomed to managing their own lives. Unfortunately, emancipation was given unwittingly by their mother while they were young. Their father's absence made it easy to predict how he thought teenage girls should be raised: 'Leave them alone, and let them do their own thing.'

"My ideas about child rearing were not what anyone expected. I believe that I, and their mother, should play an active a role in decision-making. Parents are consulted prior to a decision being made, not after the girls have finalized their plans."

"Can you provide an example of the problems you're describing?" I asked.

"For breakfast on Thursday morning, I made one of the girl's favorite meals: waffles and bacon. However, they wouldn't get out of bed.

"Eventually, I put the food in the refrigerator and proceeded to clean up the kitchen. I called up the stairs and threatened the girls with the loss of their phones if I didn't hear from them soon. Then, I said that it's not polite to ignore an adult when they are talking to you.

"Their simultaneous response was, 'you can't do that!'

"I feel so juvenile arguing with teens, but I don't think that I have a choice. I am tired of them being rude," Bill said with an exasperated sigh.

"Where was their mother during this altercation? What were her thoughts on the matter?" I asked.

"Barbara was at Publix shopping for supper. When she came home, I explained to her what had happened, that they took an attitude with me, so I took their phones, that I was tired of the disrespect. She claimed to not know what I was talking about.

"I didn't understand how she could not see it, and I still don't, but I explained it to her as best as I could. I told her that whenever I talk to them or ask one of them a question, I often get no response. I told her that they have this same attitude much of the time and that I consider their attitude disrespectful. Barbara agreed with me and asked why I didn't come to her with the problem sooner."

"That is a valid question, Bill," I said. "Perhaps we need to work on your communication skills as a couple. I know it can be hard to try and parent someone else's children, but if you two are open about the issues you face, that will help immensely."

"I agree with you, Dr. Trattoria. It's just hard when I feel as though I am a Johnny-come-lately. I didn't want to risk being the odd man out."

"Did you tell her how you felt?"

"Yes, I did. She said we should settle the issue right now and had the girls come down to the kitchen for a family meeting. She said, 'Bill tells me that you have been disrespectful to him, and I won't stand for it. You will not ignore him when he speaks to you. Do you hear me?'

"Looking like whipped puppies, they tried to minimize the role they played in the scenario. To my surprise though, neither of the girls completely denied what they did. Both girls did apologize, claiming they didn't mean to be rude."

"Well it certainly sounds like your family is at least trying, which is an important first step. Unfortunately, we are almost out of time for today, but I'll see you next week with your whole family.

"Remember the key to communication is not to hold on to it till you are ready to bust."

"I have another issue that was bothering me," Bill said.

I checked my watch. "Please go ahead. We have another few minutes before your session is over."

"When the girls have plans to do something, it would be better if they ask permission first. They assume that if they had plans, they can do whatever they please without asking permission. I feel this is wrong, and it pisses me off."

"How does Barbara feel about that?"

"She told them that when they start paying the rent, utility bills and buying food, they can make decisions.

"The kids became defensive, and Leah said, 'Ma that's silly. We can't do that. We don't have a job or money to pay for those things. Besides that's what our child support is for.'

"This was a trigger for me. I decided to question their feelings of entitlement and said, 'Maybe you need to consider what you do have. You have what you need and more. You owe us respect and that includes asking for the things you need and want.'"

"How did that go over with Barbara and the girls?" I asked.

"Barbara chimed in and said it was her fault things had gotten so out of control, that she had been feeling guilty for divorcing their father and tried to make up for it by giving them freedom. I decided to end the conversation there until after dinner. We didn't need to fight in front of the girls."

"That was a good decision," I said. "Did you guys continue discussing this later?"

"Yes, I had to share my thoughts with Barbara. I told her that as long as she allows the girls to do their own thing, she will have a battle for control with them.

"She said that she does set limits on the girls. Unfortunately, I failed to see her defensives intensify and pushed the envelope. I said that she doesn't set limits very often. She never asks where they are going, who they are with, or when they'll be home.

"Her response was, 'This isn't a prison; this is their home. I trust them, and I don't need to question everything they do.'

"Barbara was not the only defensive person in the room. I had to do a double take and try to make the suggestion in another way."

"I told her, that's not what I'm saying. Being diligent is what a parent is obligated to do to protect their children. They don't know how to protect themselves from predators, which come in all shapes, sizes, and sexual persuasions.

"Being able to shut up and listen is not my strong suit. I gave up on insisting that their mother meet their friends and their families. My view is too old-fashioned for them, although I am trying to keep the kids safe."

"You aren't incorrect about this, but everyone has different parenting styles. You and Barbara just need to get on the same page with your styles and expectations. It sounds as though you love the girls as your own, which is a necessary first step."

"I do love them, but the usual problems of disrespect and uncontrolled venting of anger against their mother causes arguments between the kids and me. When things are going well for the girls and their mother, it is easy to support them in whatever they want to do. Neither Barbara nor the girls like, accept, or understand the meaning of the word 'no!' In spite of the differences between Barbara and me, the family remains cohesive, although it is a bumpy ride."

*   *   *

FOLLOWING MY SESSION with Bill, I arranged to have the family all come in for a joint session. I offered to see them as soon as possible, but it was two weeks before they could come in. Bill was the most anxious about the meeting. He wasn't sure how he would handle the confrontation without losing control of his temper. As everyone settled into the small office, I made my initial observations.

Leah was a carbon copy of her mother in looks and temperament.

Crystal apparently takes after her father, quiet and obtuse.

To break the tension, I tried adding humor to the meeting. "I assume you all know one another?" I said with a smile.

They all laughed.

"Good morning to you all. Ladies, I am happy to finally make your acquaintance. After speaking with your mother and stepfather, I feel as though I already know you!

"Before we get started, I'd like to lay down some ground rules for the session. It's important that everyone has their chance to fully explain their perspectives without fear of interruption from other members of the family. This will allow the meeting to be its most productive and for everyone to feel as though they are being heard."

All four members of the family nodded their agreement.

"Great! Let's get this session started. Now girls, your stepfather seems to feel that you have a problem communicating. How do you feel about this?"

Leah was the first to respond. "I don't think there is a problem talking with him. His problem is that he wants to run everything. He gets testy when he doesn't get what he wants."

At this, Bill started to speak. Before he could begin, I reiterated the rules of the session. "Please remember that everyone will have their chance to speak and to respond." Bill nodded his agreement and settled back into the chair. I continued my discussion with Leah and Crystal.

"It sounds as though you see him taking over the family. But from whom, your mother or you two?" I asked.

"Mom! She gives in to him all the time. She never hears our side of an issue. It's like the problem we had over asking permission to do things. I don't see anything wrong with us assuming that we can do the things we want without asking permission," Leah said. "Mom never used to mind."

Crystal finally joined the conversation. "There are some things we should ask for, like buying something or going out of town with friends. But most of the time, we can make decisions without their help as long as we are home by curfew!"

I interrupted her monologue. "Maybe it's not a matter of asking permission but a matter of being courteous and letting them know what you are doing. Putting the shoe on the other foot, how would feel if your parents left the house and did not tell you when they would be home?"

Leah looked first to her sister for support and then to her mother.

Barbara took the cue and joined the conversation. "Dr. Trattoria is right, girls. It's simply a matter of being courteous and respectful. There's nothing wrong with asking these questions."

"I would like a chance to speak, if that's alright," Bill said, looking to Barbara, Crystal, and Leah. "How do you feel about me joining the family?"

No one saw this question coming. The girls were quiet for a few minutes, obviously thinking about how to respond.

Crystal was the first to speak up. "I like Bill. Who else would make us waffles and bacon every Thursday? I don't show my appreciation often, and I don't like all that he has to say all the time. But I'm a teenager, for heaven's sake! Give me a break!"

At this point, everyone broke into laughter.

By the end of the conversation, there were no obvious rumpled feathers. A therapeutic circle appeared to have been formed. We decided that a weekly session for the whole family would be best, as it would allow all family members to express their feelings in a safe place.

Family therapy is not the solution to all of their problems. It has its place in the grand scheme of things. Just like EMDR has its rewards when used appropriately. Sometimes a shovel is needed to dig a hole. Other times it takes a backhoe to do the job; you have to understand what you're treating.

Chapter 5

A Home is Not a Home

Two Oceans Nursing home is typical of nursing homes in rural North Carolina. It's a two-story yellow brick building that is surrounded by crepe myrtle trees and azaleas. The front of the building faces the street, and the parking lot is off the back.

After parking my car, I walked around to the front of the building and rang the doorbell. A security guard buzzed me through and asked me to present my credentials. Once inside, I walked to the nurse's station and asked to see the patient.

"Is Gloria Williams available to be interviewed? I'm Dr. Trattoria, and I'm here to see Ms. Williams for her annual mental health exam. It was requested by Dr. Ayers, her primary doctor."

"We were not aware of your appointment, but she can be seen shortly," the ward clerk answered.

"Great, thank you. Is the social worker on the unit?" I asked.

"No, sir," she answered. "Mrs. Wicker is not currently on the unit, but she is in the building. I'll page her for you. Please give me one moment to get Gloria's medical records for you," she said, getting up and walking to the shelves of files behind her.

After a few minutes spent looking for "Williams, Gloria," she finally found the thick stack of files.

"Here you are, sir," she said, handing me the files through the window.

Just the thickness alone confirmed that Ms. Williams had been in the facility for some time. It would take hours to read through them and to digest the material. Wicker could have summarized the findings in less time, but I had nothing else to do while I waited for her to arrive and began skimming the material.

When the social worker arrived about 20 minutes later, she was friendly and approachable, as you would expect a person in her position to be.

"Good morning, how can I be of service to you?" said Mrs. Wicker.

"I'm here to interview Gloria Williams. I didn't have a chance to finish reading her medical records, as they're extensive. What can you tell me about her?"

"Well, it's going to be impossible to interview her."

"What do you mean? I was told by the ward clerk that I would be able to see her today."

"She wasn't mistaken; you will be able to meet with her, but an interview will prove difficult. Gloria lost her speech a year ago as a result of a stroke.

"She was diagnosed as receptive and expressive aphasic. Complicating her care further, she lost her vision due to the stroke about six months ago. The neurologist reported she had a dozen or more TIAs."

"Does Gloria have many visitors?" I asked.

"You're the first visitor she has had in months. Her medical records are the only source of information we have. I don't know what you're looking for, but there isn't a lot of information in the chart, despite its size."

"I would like to know what her life was like before all the neurological problems."

"I may not be able to answer that. Gloria had been a patient here for the better part of four years before I was hired. The staff pieced together her social history as best they could from incidental visitors. Her records do not indicate that she was ever married or gave birth. I remember reading that she completed 7th grade."

"I'll take all the records you can find. Maybe there is something that has been overlooked that may prove helpful."

*   *   *

AFTER SPENDING SEVERAL hours reading her chart, I found a leaf in her family tree. I thought I had uncovered a piece of her history, one that was surprisingly overlooked.

I reported my findings to Mrs. Wicker.

"Gloria was married once, and she had a daughter. There is no record of where the family came from and nothing to indicate that she had visitors. The records named her child's father as Howard Trueborn. It was during her first commitment that he broke off all connection with her.

"When he abandoned her, she seemed broken and stopped trying to help herself. Gloria quit trying to manage the expenses. Her daughter was turned over to social services to be raised in foster homes. There was no mention of the child in her records after she was placed in the system. It was like she disappeared without a trace. I can't believe that you missed this piece of her history."

Mrs. Wicker didn't have much new to say in response to my findings. With no family or interested party to invest time with Gloria, she was shoved to the back burner. That's life in a nursing home.

I was finally brought to Gloria's room and was confronted with a woman who appeared to be asleep. She laid in her bed with her eyes closed. There was no indication that she was aware that I or anyone was in the room with her. After 15 minutes of trying to elicit a response unsuccessfully, I left.

It wasn't that long ago when going to work ignited my day. I felt needed and appreciated, as if I served a purpose greater than myself.

I never thought of work as entertainment, but it was an exciting distraction. Sleepless nights dull my wits and make problem-solving a chore.

There was a time when performing my services as a forensic psychologist was routinely applauded. The daily challenge for me was becoming one of managing my cynicism in dealing with the public, with people like Mrs. Wicker, who don't appear to give a damn about the patients in their care. If they didn't care, who would?

I decided it was time to call my friend.

"Aaron, how are you doing? It's 4 o'clock somewhere in the north east." This is an arbitrary standard that we employed to gauge if we were alcoholics. Anyone who drinks before 4 p.m. must be an alcoholic, right?

"How do you feel about getting a beer or two at Smokey's?" I asked.

"I have some errands to run. As soon as I get them out of the way, I'll join you for a celebration. Probably about an hour," Aaron responded.

"Great, see you then."

*   *   *

I ARRIVED AT the gin mill 30 minutes early. It's the first time I'd been there in years. No one looked familiar, so I took a seat on a tall bar stool in the center of the room. It's hard to say how many of the patrons would react to a psychologist. My glasses are a giveaway, round and rimless; they look like something worn by professors or pseudointellectuals. I haven't made up my mind if I'm one or the other. Sometimes I have misgivings about who I am or who I'm supposed to be.

Life experiences have taught me not to take anything for granted. Just when things seem to be going great, someone will throw a monkey wrench at you. If it is not your health that is taken away, it's someone you love who is taken from you. Just look at what happened to Gloria. She had issues with her mental health and was abandoned by her family, her daughter taken from her care.

Sometimes life just seems unfair.

Chapter 6
One Note Does Not a Composition Make

Patients who call for an appointment generally come by themselves. When they come in with a family member, they frequently have an agenda and are seeking something other than treatment for themselves.

The relationship between a child and a parent is one such common scenario. It takes time for me to build trust with each of them. If the relationship is solid, it can work to the advantage of both parent and child and make the job easier for the therapist. When the parent trusts the therapist, the child has a sense that they can trust him too. During the time it takes for trust to develop, the results are sometimes specular. My work is like a musical chord that has no meaning apart from the rest of the composition. Every party at play must contribute hard work, time, and risk to be successful.

Karen Callaghan called for an appointment for her 14-year-old daughter. According to Karen, Rene, her daughter, had been a poster child of the perfect teenage girl. She was respectful, honest, and a studious. Rene was never involved with street drugs or alcohol. Her mother said she could be trusted and always does as she is told.

"Why do you want your daughter seen?" I asked.

"Something just isn't right. I can't tell you exactly what is wrong, but I have a feeling that something isn't right," Karen said. "Call it a mother's intuition."

"Okay, why don't you two come in next Monday morning at 9."

"Thank you, Dr. Trattoria."

*   *   *

THE MORNING OF the appointment, I could hear the mother and daughter arguing in the waiting room.

"I told you to dress down for the appointment, not give up all manner of civility," Karen said, lashing out at her daughter.

"Well I told you not to make the appointment to see a shrink! He has nothing to add to the conversation that we don't ready know," Rene said, her voice rising in frustration.

Karen was attractive and stylishly dressed in a pair of slacks and a white blouse. Her hair was cut short and her language usage suggested average intelligence.

Rene was dressed like a typical teen, frayed jeans and a man's plaid shirt. She appeared poised and confident, making her appear older than 14.

After making my initial observances, I decided to chime in before the fight got out of control.

"Hello ladies. Allow me to introduce myself. I'm Dr. Trattoria. Why don't you step into my office, so we can keep this meeting confidential?"

The women stopped bickering long enough to follow me into the office. Rene sat with her arms crossed and as far from her mother as she could while still being in the room. It was obvious to me that

I needed to build trust with Rene if I wanted this meeting to be successful.

Before coming in, I had asked Karen for some basic family information. I learned that Karen had sole custody, but that recently, Rene began spending every other weekend with her stepmother and father.

"Now what is all of the squabbling about?" I asked, getting settled into my own chair.

"Rene is annoyed because I made this appointment to see you," Karen said.

"I see. And what is the reason for this appointment?" I asked. I pointedly directed the question to both women, hoping to see who took over the conversation.

"I don't know what's wrong with her," Rene said, refusing to make eye contact with me or her mother. "I don't have any issues that I can't figure out by myself."

Karen appeared mortified by the way Rene talked in front of me.

"Your mother has all of the right reasons for making the appointment," I said. "She just cares about your well-being. Isn't that right, Karen?"

She gave a curt nod before diving into her diatribe.

"You have been moody and closed off the last few weeks. I think it has something to do with spending weekends at your father's. It could be how you spend your time with your friends or maybe even your stepmother, as your father appears to have a limited role with what is going on at his house."

"Is she right about that?" I asked Rene.

"What makes you think there is a problem at Dad's house?" Rene said, not answering my question.

"The problems did not begin till you started spending weekends at his house."

"I'm fine. This has nothing to do with Dad," Rene said.

I decided to jump in here and try to steer the conversation in a peaceful direction.

"Your mother didn't say it has anything to do with your father. It's understandable that you're defensive of him, given the recent custody issues. Split families can be difficult to navigate.

"The only thing she said was that the problem was linked to the time you spend at his home. Perhaps, you can tell your mother and I what has changed in the last few weeks. Your mother is concerned for you because she loves you."

My efforts to gain Rene's trust appeared to be working. She looked visibly more relaxed than when she had entered my office. Her arms were no longer crossed, and she was leaning toward her mother and I as we all spoke about how she spent her weekends at her father's house and the friends she made in the neighborhood.

"I'm in love with Sam, and I believe he loves me too," Rene blurted out, looking at her mother for approval. "I'm sorry I didn't tell you, but I knew you wouldn't approve."

"What makes you think that Sam's in love with you? And why wouldn't your mother approve?" I asked.

"He just can't get enough of me. And it's not just sex; he cares for me," Rene said.

At the mention of sex, Karen got a panicked look on her face. I quickly gave her a subtle signal to keep quiet and let her daughter continue.

"He's the first man who has asked me what I think. He wants to know what I think about Obama, Ferguson, the war, everything."

"What do you do besides watch TV and lay in bed?" I asked.

"Well, nothing if you discount watching Anderson Cooper and CNN. I can't help it if we have sex; it's part of a relationship."

Tears threatened at this point, but she held them back and continued.

"I guess we travel everywhere in the world with CNN," she said wistfully.

"It sounds like you think Sam is shallow and that your relationship seems to only revolve around sex. Is that all you want to say?" I asked.

"That's not what I said," Rene said defensively.

"It might not have been what you said, but it seems like you know this is true, even if you don't want to admit it."

"You've got that right," Karen said with a look toward her daughter. "I know you want to believe that he's different. Unfortunately, some men only care about sex."

* * *

TWO WEEKS LATER, I had a follow-up appointment with Rene and her mother. Karen claimed that her daughter was a changed person and was back to acting like the daughter she knew.

There was no reason to discuss her romantic interlude with Sam. At the end of the joint session, I ask for a brief meeting with Rene alone. Grateful to have her daughter back in her life, her mother agreed.

"So, Rene, what did you learn from CNN this week?" I asked without cracking a smile.

"You know, without my bed pal, I can't say that I missed too much in the news. He never called me to see what was going on with me, why I stopped calling him and coming over. I don't believe it was my brain he was interested in. If someone wants to know what is new in the news, they can turn on their TV."

All was well with Rene, and she learned something about men. Not all of my patients consider me a sympathetic listener. Rene missed the validation of her personal worth through my attention to their every word.

Doing what is right sometimes leaves me with the appearance of being dangerously insightful. My attention to detail and the recognition of incongruous thoughts and feelings help me recognize what is camouflage and what is real in my patient's stories.

It is only on rare occasions that patients acknowledge what I am doing and even rarer that they recognize that it is their own accomplishment. I can't help being a teacher, and I accomplish my lesson plans at conscious and unconscious levels. My patient's attitudes change as if by magic. They acquire the ability to be self-nurturing and self-forgiving, often without knowing how it is accomplished. That is my trademark.

My search for virtue and what's best in my fellow man is pursued through a Socratic style of inquiry. I make it my business to help others become honest, if with no one but themselves.

The effort to get my patients to achieve honesty is an up-hill battle, much like the mythical struggle of Sisyphus rolling an immense bolder up a hill.

There are times when the effort to provide insight to my patients becomes a dialogue like that of a dance instructor. It's two steps forward and one step back. Sometimes the footwork becomes entangled, and patients get frustrated, angry, and despairing, thinking that the task is beyond them. Patients who acquire a sense of helplessness fail to believe in themselves because the dialogue cannot be deciphered.

When a client opens himself up to the interaction with me, he experiences a transformation. This permits the didactic message to change to an emotional connection. Over the course of two or three visits, the client disowns his insight, which is full of rationalizing displaced anger and resentment.

Other times, I might run into a therapeutic block. Occasionally the patient throws in the towel and gives up on the idea of therapeutic intervention. The treatment ends abruptly. In these cases, I respond differently.

Like the matador in the bull ring, I become completely focused on the problem. I don't confuse the charging bull with the patient seeking my care. In an analogous vein, I take on the character of Cervantes' Don Quixote and continue to do the right thing for my patient.

I stick to my strategy and tenacious adherence to my Socratic method. The client's fears become tolerable and conquerable. Imagined dragons turn out to be old windmills and unconquerable foes reveal flaws to be exploited. Words that sort out the client's confusion, which frighten and upset them, become the elixir. This elixir allows the client to not only tolerate the truth but provide them with an insatiable need to know all there is to know.

In most cases, clients succeed without psychotropic medication or the need for in-patient hospitalizations. In the first few sessions, I do my best to discover who the client is and to have the client discover who they are. Time spent building trust and modeling honesty are the foundations upon which I build my cognitive highway. It is my bedrock for moving the client from point A to point B.

Chapter 7

Mike Nary Is Not Pro Bono

It was mid-morning, and my phone would not quit ringing. Unfortunately, Sophie had the day off, and I had to cover the office phones, transcribe my progress notes, and see a few patients. My only defense against the ringing was to pick up the receiver and talk to whoever was on the other end of the line.

"My name is Mike Nary. I'm sorry for bothering you, but I need to see you as soon as possible."

I didn't recognize the voice and realized it must be someone seeking a new doctor.

"Well Mr. Nary, what kind of dilemma produced your urgency?"

"I can't take Lucy's threats any longer. I've done nothing to deserve her abuse, but I don't know what I can do to stop it."

The desperation in his voice coupled with the intensity of the feelings signaled to me that he was desperate and confused.

"Are you or Lucy in any danger of hurting yourself or someone else?" I asked.

"No, I'm not a threat to anyone, including myself. I can't take Lucy's smothering this way. How much more of her intrusive behavior am I expected to take?" Mike explained. "She is having a difficult time dealing with me losing my job. I could better understand her situation if we were having serious financial hardships, but that is not the case."

"What is it she expects you to do? It sounds as if she's the one with the problems."

"Well, you know what they say: if mamma isn't happy, no one is happy."

"What will it take to make 'mamma' happy?" I asked him.

"I don't know," Mike replied.

"Are you and Lucy married? How long have you and Lucy been together?" I asked hoping to learn more about the couple.

"Yes, we have been married for 47 years. We have no children. That was a condition she had prior to getting married," Mike said.

"Have you had issues in the past?" I asked.

"Yes, 15 years ago she said she wanted out of the marriage. Nothing came of it because Lucy changed her mind within a week. I can't say that we reconciled fully, but there was never a formal separation and neither of us got lawyer."

"What was the issue 15 years ago?"

"When I asked her why she wanted a divorce, she said that she needed a change. I don't know any more now than I knew the first time she said she wanted to separate.

"She came home, and nothing was ever said about it. I didn't challenge her rational. Maybe I should have, but I was afraid she would change her mind. I have a feeling that she gets tired of being married. The grass is greener on the other side of the fence, and she needs her freedom."

"So, what do you think the issue is now?" I asked.

"This is the first time I have been unemployed in 16 years. My wife says she can't take the pressure of the bills, but we don't have much outstanding debt.

"My company gave me the choice of resigning or getting fired, and I told them they would have to fire me. If I resigned, there was a chance of losing my benefits. The choice was a no-brainer. I'm frugal, and so is my wife. We have no debt other than our mortgage. Lucy works as a legal secretary. Her reasoning just doesn't make sense."

"Maybe it isn't your unemployment that has her worked up. It could it be something else," I suggested.

"You're right," Mike agreed. "I must be missing something, so I need help finding answers. I still have my health insurance, so that will help pay for my appointment."

"I'd be happy help" I said. "I have an opening next Monday. My office manager is out today, but she will give you a call in the morning to get your insurance information and preauthorization, along with an estimate of the co-pay."

* * *

THE NEXT MORNING, Sophie called me into her office in between appointments.

"You know Mike Nary, the man who called yesterday? He's on the line. He is having a difficult time deciding if you are worth $75 an hour," she said.

"I have to charge something for my services. It sounds like whatever I charge would be too much. I get so angry when I consider the relative costs for services. The plumber demands $75 an hour to unclog the toilet, and he wants me to fix his marriage for less?"

"A damn handyman is going to hit you up for $150 an hour to install a prefab door from Lowes. You didn't spend 35 years with your nose in books to learn his job," Sophie said, adding salt to the wound without even thinking.

"You're damn right! Is the handyman going to get sued for using two-inch screws instead of galvanized nails? If he uses my job to advertise his skills in the local paper, is there any recourse? But when a client calls in pursuit of professional advice about himself and his wife, my advice is supposed to be offered pro bono?" I said with indignation.

"Hell no!" Sophie said, snorting with laughter.

We both heard a faint "hello?" coming from the receiver. I quickly realized that the prospective client was still on the phone; Sophie had mistakenly not put him on hold, and he had been listening to us spout off.

At this point, I knew that the client was lost, even if I had wanted him. I decided to play a little game with him and picked up the phone.

"Good morning, Mr. Nary. I understand you are questioning the value of my services," I said calmly.

"You are a self-serving son-of-a- bitch, and you should rot in hell!" Mike said, expressing his contempt with vitriolic disclosure.

"I assume this means that you will be looking for someone else to answer your need for help, then? Good to hear. Goodbye now," I said and hung up the phone.

This verbal exchange relieved me of any professional obligation to provide services to this wolverine in man's clothing. Not everyone seeking professional services expresses sentiments with such transparency.

No one wants to pay their bill, and nearly all my clients look for a way out of managing their expenses. The insurance companies do not feel it is their problem, and every issue is explained away as a pre-existing condition. Everyone wants my services pro bono.

Chapter 8
Margaret Wearing

It's 5:15 in the evening, and the late afternoon light coming through the wooden blinds cast shadows that darkened the room. I was sitting in my high-backed chair trying not to stare at the wall clock through eyes that were at half-mast. The day had taken its toll, and my strength and patience had all but run out.

At this point, I was looking for an opportunity to end the last clinical interview of the day. I have learned to recognized when it is time to say good night. A tell-tale sign is when I listen to my patients without hearing them or feeling their emotions.

My last patient of the day was Margaret Wearing, a 54-year-old patient who was looking to resolve her problem with depression, a problem that is intensified by loneliness and interpersonal avoidance. Professional decorum prevented me from broadcasting my honest thoughts regarding the session, but I sure wished it didn't.

Margaret, you haven't stopped talking for 47 minutes. For the past six sessions you have screamed, cried, and complained that no one loves you. Would you say there is a pattern here? I get the feeling that your external behavior is one of the factors creating distance between you and the people who know you.

I changed my position to better make eye contact with Margaret. I needed to stay focused for the remainder of the session, or at least appear that way. Regardless of how I sat in the chair, visual contact with Margaret was fleeting and quickly broken.

*   *   *

IN A VIRTUAL reality environment, a computer is used to create sensations that are audible and visual. These phenomena, referred to as immersion, hinge on the quality of the telepathic medium and its capacity to enhance perceptual distortion electronically. Immersion is capable of giving someone the feeling of being part of another world and to be able to interact with it in a meaningful way. Even without a computer, Margaret was able to transform her clinical hour in a modestly decorated office into a romantic interlude with her psychologist.

Margaret filled me in to what was happening in her mind during the session, and I was horrified.

"You had your way with me. I recall you kissing me and running your hand up my legs. I recall your heavy breathing, and you being on top of me," Margaret said.

"If I can prove to you that those events never happened, what would you say?"

"How would you do that?"

"Remember the paper you signed giving me permission to tape these sessions? I have the session on video recording. Your session was taped. There was no romantic interlude. I have to refute your story with the recorded version of the truth. There was no romantic event as you imagined it."

The combination of sensing you are somewhere other than where you are and interacting with it in meaningful ways is called telepresence. This seemed to explain what Margaret was experiencing. Without a computer, the same phenomena and the same perceptual experiences are defined as psychosis, replete with delusions and hallucinations. To call therapy a virtual reality is to misrepresent what happened in the room. Unfortunately, Margaret saw no connection between what happened and her treatment goals.

"Margaret, you have covered a great deal of painful history, not to mention our discussion about the fantasies you experienced about the session. You must be exhausted. I suggest that we stop at this point and resume next week."

"Isn't it ironic that I have become an object of indifference with someone I have come to trust and with whom I share my most intimate feelings. How do you dismiss what you let happen? I wonder if this is déjà vu or quid pro quo," Margaret said before leaving my office.

The magical healing support and compassion that are my trademarks were lost this session. I know Margaret's feelings are in turmoil. Her anger is muted by her fear of rejection and her need to be loved. The need to recover her ego turns the therapy session into a contest. Reality is sacrificed in order to win control of the clinical hour.

After the session ended, I realized that getting through to her is like beating my head against a stone wall. I need to call my friend Aaron, a fellow psychologist, for ideas on how to get through to Margaret.

"Hi Aaron, do you have about a few moments to talk about a patient?" I asked. "She's really got me scratching my head."

"Should I put you on the clock?" he asked.

"This is pro bono," I said, and we both laughed.

"So, what is on your mind, Tony?"

"I have a patient who has me wondering what I can do to help her. I have tried to suggest that she can manage her fear of intimacy without any change in behavior. I tried to use wakeful hypnotic suggestions to help her manage her fears, albeit unsuccessfully. I attempted to incorporate her into small group sessions, which she rejected.

"Modeling communication skills and behavioral rehearsal have proven only marginally successful. She still refuses to use her acquired skills. I am at a loss to know how to infuse courage into this client."

"There isn't going to be a quick fix. Time, patience and the willingness to indulge her need for self-reassurance is what is needed. Do you have what it takes to fix her?" Aaron asked.

"My unconditional acceptance and emotional support seem to be the only intervention Margaret is willing to accept. I worry about her emotional dependency and attachment to me. Margaret is aware of this attachment. Her attraction to me is all that she recognizes."

"That is the burden mental health practitioners take on when they enter a therapeutic alliance with a character disorder," Aaron said.

While you're correct, I worry about this case in particular. Our relationship has become a real fantasy for Margaret. She is not able to define the parameters of her fantasies. Unless I can convince her of the scope of her fantasies, I cannot gauge the extent of her dissociative experiences. This makes it difficult to guide her back into the real world and dangerous for me. Margaret represents a threat to my license to practice psychology. I need to transfer her to someone who isn't a part of her fantasy world."

"What if I were to step up and assume responsibly for her care, how would that work for you?" Aaron asked.

"I would appreciate that, but who's to say that you would not become the object of her fantasy?"

"No one, but there will be a paper trail that will document that you did everything you could to discourage the fantasy. I don't know what more you can do."

"I would appreciate your help with Margaret. I will have to do as you suggest and end my treatment. I will have a meeting with her on Monday, and that should be it. I'll arrange to have her call your office. Once again, I don't know how to thank you."

Chapter 9

"Life is but a Dream"

"He's got to be nuts," Sergeant Moore said as he pulled up to the scene. "He's got nothing but a t-shirt on and is holding his penis in his right hand."

Sergeant Moore exited the patrol car and made his way to the group of officers gathered in a cluster.

"Can someone give me a quick summary?' Sergeant Moore asked.

"Anytime cars were stopped at the red light, the perpetrator would approach the driver's side window, wave his penis at the driver, and solicit sexual favors. This happened over and over again for 15 to 20 minutes, affecting three dozen drivers or so," Brian Lott, the arresting officer, said. "The perpetrator became increasingly frustrated and angry as drivers ignored him and refused to lower their windows. He became aggressive as his frustration turned to anger. He started hitting the windows and screaming profanities.

"Eventually someone called 9-1-1 after a larger black lady got out of her car and swung her pocketbook like it was a baseball bat. I don't know if there is any connection between this woman and the perpetrator, but her reaction indicates that there is one.

"It was much more difficult to subdue the perpetrator given his nudity.

Worse yet, he became sexually aroused during the take-down. His penis was hanging mid-way between his hips and his knee, looking more like a club than a body part. The picture of three men in blue uniforms rolling on the ground with the perpetrator looked like a scene out of a Woody Allen movie. The cameras didn't make the fight any easier. I'm sure there will be some videos on the evening news."

"And the woman who swung at him, what happened to her?" Sergeant Moore asked.

"She had to be restrained. She eventually calmed down. She's in the patrol car over there," Officer Lott said with a nod.

"Did anyone read him his Miranda rights?" Sergeant Moore asked.

"Before or after he got his erection? That looked like a lethal weapon!" Brian Lott said, to which they all laughed.

*   *   *

ONCE THEY HAD transported the perpetrator to the jail, he cooperated.

Amanda Kessler and five additional correction officers did a cursory body search on the prisoner and got him into a yellow jumpsuit and prison sandals.

In the blink of an eye, he was naked again and threatening to have sex with Amanda and two of the correction officers. Amanda was not a wilting lily. At 5 foot 10 inches tall and nearly 230 pounds, she can manage most men if it comes to a physical confrontation.

After he was wrangled back into his jumpsuit, the perpetrator approached a male correction officer and offered him a blow job. He was escorted to seclusion.

"This guy is nuts," said Sergeant Moore, the shift commander. "I don't know what the magistrate will do, but we better get a competency assessment lined up. Who would you recommend?"

"With such short notice, Dr. Trattoria is the first one who comes to mind," Officer Kessler said.

"I was told he had retired," replied Sergeant Wilcox. "It can't hurt to call him and find out. He does a decent forensic assessment, but the perpetrator's attorney may have his own ideas about who he wants to do the forensic examination."

Amanda Kessler put a call into the assistant district attorney to find out who would be representing George Sullivan. He is homeless, has no job, and is not a licensed driver. It was obvious that he could not afford his own attorney.

The public defender assigned to his case was a man by the name of Calvin Drake. He had no problem with Dr. Trattoria completing the assessment, and a call was made to schedule the interview that afternoon.

"Hello, Dr. Trattoria, this is Amanda Kessler at the county jail. I've got a genuine nut for you to examine."

"What kind of nut did you have in mind, a coconut or peanut?"

"The two-legged kind who is a danger to himself and others," Amanda retorted. "He is about to get himself killed in jail. He can't seem to stop himself from soliciting sex from anyone he comes into contact with. That can be a fatal mistake in jail."

"What was he arrested for?" I asked.

"He was originally charged with being a public nuisance and indecent exposure while soliciting sexual favors from anyone who approached him. He was also charged with assault on a government official and resisting arrest," she said.

"Have there been any other arrests?"

"About a dozen arrests in this county, all similar to what happened this afternoon. Mr. Sullivan has a habit of making a nuisance of himself," Amanda said.

"If there isn't a conflict, I can interview Mr. Sullivan tomorrow at 9 a.m."

"That will work," said Amanda.

"See you tomorrow," I replied before hanging up the receiver.

*   *   *

MY DRIVE TO the Craven County detention center was pleasant. I had no recollection of a man named George Sullivan. It is possible that I had seen him for disability determination some time ago, but there was not a glimmer of a memory I could bring to the matter.

The walk from the parking lot to the admissions building seems further every year. Beyond the door is a security room where visitors are screened prior to admission. After going through an identity search and explaining my reason for coming to the prison, I was admitted.

Inside the cell block, I was questioned again by the guards about the reason for my visit. I responded with a pleasant smile and an explanation before being led to my destination. There were no pleasant greetings from the guards inside the cell block. A few of the prisoners were doing their assigned jobs in a perfunctory way. The walls smelled of strong detergent, having been washed with a bleach solution several hours ago.

We soon reached the administrative wing. The names of the administrators were on the wall above the door. Amanda Kessler's appeared prominently, along with her job title. Her office was closed, as is customary.

I knocked twice, and the command was given to enter. In the office, behind a mountain of files, sat a large woman dressed in a grey prison uniform.

She rose slowly to greet me and reached across her desk to shake my hand.

"Good morning, Dr. Trattoria. I am happy to see you. It's been a while since I've had the opportunity to work with you. I'm glad to see that the rumor of your retirement was a mistake."

"I don't know how the rumor got started. I guess it had something to do with my age," I said with a smile. "I hear Mr. Sullivan has been raising everyone's anxiety, inmates and correction officers alike."

"Are you blessed with ESP or am I missing something here? I knew we picked the right shrink for the job. How did you know about the correction officers?" she asked.

"I saw the news last night and figured if he was beating the hell out of street cops, the correction officers would have their work cut out for them. Besides, one night at this bed and breakfast wouldn't straighten him up. The correction officers only provided him with playmates."

"Don't tell that to the correction officers," she advised. "The inmate's records are arranged in chronological order. The most recent are on top. Do you have any questions?"

"I assume that his attorney has been informed of my coming to see him?" I asked.

"Mr. Drake signed off on you completing his forensic examination."

"Great. I'm sure I'll have plenty of questions later," I responded.

* * *

AFTER I WAS escorted to an empty office space reserved for people like myself, I flipped open the top file. I found an entry note made by the prison nurse, Ms. Wallace: "The prisoner was agitated and highly excitable, and I could not understand his gibberish. George was also talking to others in the room when no one was there.

"The nurse made a decision to give the inmate a shot of Haldol to bring his 'psychosis' under control, which he refused. The nurse told him that he was going to seclusion and had no say in the matter. He tried to bully the nurse in an effort to talk his way out the shot, but it did not work.

"After Ms. Wallace pressed the needle into his right buttock, Sullivan paused for fewer than 20 seconds before he spun himself around, grabbed his penis and said, 'Would you like some of this?'

"George was restrained in less time than it took for his pants to hit the floor and was escorted to his cell."

My reading was interrupted by a group of correction officers who escorted Mr. Sullivan to the interview room. He was dressed in a bright yellow jumpsuit and was wearing a full complement of security hardware: hand cuffs, waist shackle, and leg irons. It was easy to imagine the staff preparing me to interview Hannibal Lector.

Wearing wire-rimmed glasses, the small framed black man reminded me of comedian Red Foxx when he played Fred Sanford in the 1960s comedy *Sanford and Son.*

He was walking with a limp, a consequence of his interactions with security. While George was standing at attention in all of the shackles, I asked the guards if all the precautions are necessary.

"It's up to you how much security is needed," the senior guard said.

I looked to George. "Do you think you can behave yourself for the next 40 minutes?"

George answered the question with a few questions of his own. "Who are you? Why am I seeing you?"

"I will introduce myself, but first you need to answer my question."

"Alright, but you'll have to repeat the question. What did you ask?"

"George, you have to pay better attention to what's going on around you. Do you think you can behave yourself for the next 40 minutes? Yes or no?" By laying the ground rules for the interview, I was hoping to take control of the conversation.

"What if the answer is yes, do I get some kind of prize?"

"Well, we can remove the cuffs and shackles," I responded. "Is that enough incentive for you to behave?"

"Yes, yes, a thousand times YES," George shouted with panic in his voice, clearly afraid that the opportunity had passed.

"Alright then," I said and instructed the correction officers to remove both the handcuffs and shackles.

"Are you sure you want both handcuffs and shackles off of the inmate?" the guard asked, appearing somewhat confused.

"Yes, certainly," I insisted. "When you have taken the hardware off, you can leave the room."

Within minutes, George was 25 pounds lighter. When the last guard passed through the door, George felt safe to begin talking.

"I don't think you're playing with a full deck," he remarked.

"You prefer it the other way, with chains and shackles? We can do it that way if you'd like."

"No!"

"You gave me your word that you would control yourself for 40 minutes. Are you telling me now that you can't keep it together?" I asked.

"No, but how do you know that I'm telling the truth?" George asked.

"I don't. The truth will be obvious to us at the end of 40 minutes. One of us has to take the chance to see what the facts are, and you have more to lose than I do."

George became quiet and waited for me to make the next move.

"You asked why I'm seeing you. I'm here at the request of your attorney to do a competency assessment on you. In other words, the court wants me to tell them if your elevator goes to the top floor. Now to be fair, not many people have elevators that make it to the top floor, but if yours falls somewhere between the fourth and fifth floors, that would be helpful."

"I don't know what the fuck you're talking about," George said.

"Tell me what you were doing naked in the middle of Highway 70."

"I wasn't naked. I had a T-shirt and boots on," George said.

"Okay, what were you doing in the in the middle of Highway 70 half-naked?" I asked. "Is that your version of having your elevator close to the top floor?"

"I don't know about the elevator, but I thought I might be lucky and find me a lady to love for a few hours," George responded.

"Did you really expect to meet a sexual partner in the middle of the highway?"

"If you don't ask, you won't ever know. Besides, I'm not built like the average man, and most woman find me special enough to spark their interest."

"Hmm. If you are interested in a female sexual partner, why did you ask the male guard if he would give you a blow job?"

"Half the planet is made up of men. I don't know why I should deny myself all that pleasure."

"So, you have no preference when it comes to having sex? Is a warm body all it takes to satisfy the need?" I asked.

"No, not all. There has to be excitement, a rush to get Jackson to come to life. Something to make it interesting."

I sought to further clarify what he was trying to say and continued to ask leading questions. "What if you're with a woman who isn't into you? How do you reach that same level of excitement?"

"If I'm with Mrs. Wholesome, I start playing rough, slapping her around. Sometimes it becomes mutually abusive till one of us loses control, and all hell breaks loose."

"What do you mean, 'all hell breaks loose?'" I asked.

"I get mad if she hurts me. Then, she changes all the rules. We go from slapping to throwing punches. Then all bets are off. It becomes exciting. I forget what I'm doing, and a fight breaks out, and she gets hurt."

"Is that the only way that you can get Jackson excited? Beat someone up?"

"Some porn gets me excited. But not just when Harry is banging Sally kind of thing. You know, you got someone playing with a kid, and they decide that they are tired of playing nice. So, they turn Stephen King loose with the kid," George said. "Maybe they burn the kid with a cigarette, and he screams and cries out in pain. That gets Jackson breathing hard. The kid is in for a rough time. Jackson gets all worked up."

I needed to know if any of his rough play has turned lethal. "Have you sent any of your partners to the hospital and/or killed any of them?"

"Well, that's two questions. Which question would like me to answer first?"

"Have you killed any of your partners?" I asked, cutting to the chase.

"I don't stick around and take their pulse, and I never sent anyone to the hospital. So, I don't know. That's not my problem," George said.

At this point, the formal testing began in earnest. As a warm up exercise, I began with a Bender Visual Motor Gestalt Test, or a Bender-Gestalt test for short. This test consists of a drawing exercise that indicates how cooperative the patient will be. It's a test of fine motor skills, not an aptitude test. The results were consistent with observations of other adults in similar circumstances, and I began administering the Wechsler Adult Intelligence Scale.

George relaxed with the block design test. This test is constructed in such a manner so that the first question of each subtest is scaled from easy to more difficult. The next three items are moderately difficult, and suddenly, we are into items that separate the men from the boys. Fortunately, the test comes to an end after just two consecutive mistakes.

The second test is language-based. It draws upon the inmate's ability to see similarities between common words. Like each of the tests, they begin pretty easy and become increasingly difficult. George began to act defensively as the mistakes piled up.

"What is this going to prove?" he asked.

"I can't discuss the test with you now, but please be patient and cooperate. I'll tell you all about it when the test is over."

"It sounds like silly shit. How are a poem and a statue alike? They are not alike. A poem is made of words, and a statue is made of stone. How could they be the same? I don't want to play this game anymore."

"It's important to your defense to make a real effort."

"Why is it important to say that I'm an idiot?" George asked, his frustration showing on his face.

I was able to calm him down and continue with the tests, although his patience was growing thinner and thinner.

By the time we reached the vocabulary test, George had all but given up, pretending that he was smarter than me.

The Rorschach personality test was next administered. It is intended to help with differential diagnosis. When George was introduced to the test, he became obviously excited.

"Where did you get all those pictures of naked ladies?" George asked.

"Why don't you show me where the naked ladies are in the blots," I said. The further the testing progressed, the less crazy he appeared to be.

It was easy to establish that George has below average intelligence, but he also has a good memory and can concentrate if he is engaged in the subject. His formal reasoning is not impaired. There is evidence of dependency, which supports the diagnosis of drugs and alcohol abuse.

There is character disorder and evidence of sexual sadism, but no evidence of a psychotic disorder. George sees no reason to exercise control over his primitive feelings, and that makes him dangerous.

*   *   *

WITHIN THREE HOURS of being back at my office, the tests were scored and interpreted, my impressions typed up and ready for his attorney.

As I reviewed the arrest record, I was struck by way the client managed the system. Each time he was arrested, he created the impression that he was crazy enough to have someone call for a mental status and competency examination. A preliminary decision was followed by a 30-day stay at one of the three psychiatric hospitals in the area.

There was no sign of an after-care plan following any of the competency assessments or extended hospital stays. He was never returned to jail or prison to finish his sentence. How did this little snake wiggle through the cracks in the system?

One thing was certain: George had not been helped by his sojourns in the hospitals, and his behavior was becoming increasingly dangerous.

I felt it was important to discuss my findings with Calvin Drake. Although I was not expecting a sympathetic listener from the overworked public defender, I decided to call him anyway.

"Good morning, Mr. Drake. This is Dr. Trattoria. I have completed the competency assessment on your client, a Mr. George Sullivan. When can you find time in your schedule to meet with me to discuss him?"

"My time is really skinny, and I don't know when I can find time to see you," Calvin said, confirming my expectations.

"I would like a face-to-face meeting with you. His diagnosis is not as easy as one would imagine," I said.

"Okay, just how crazy is he?" Drake asked.

"Like I said, it is not a black and white issue. There are some mental health issues that have not been addressed by the psychiatrists who have seen him in the past."

"You know, the best you can do is to send him to the state hospital to sort the mess out," Drake said, clearly annoyed.

"That's not been very helpful up to this point. If one thing came out of the hospitalizations, it's that he learned how inept the system is and how to take advantage of it."

"That's not your problem. All you were asked to do is decide if he can assist his counsel in his defense," Drake said.

"Aren't you concerned with how dangerous he is becoming?" I respond.

"No, I'm not, and that isn't a concern of yours either. Your report is intended to clarify whether he can assist in his defense and whether he knows right from wrong. That is all," Drake said again.

"It's not so simple to me. Doesn't it concern you that you're contributing to his sexual sadism and that he can become one of those serial fellows you see on America's Most Wanted?"

"Don't let your imagination get ahead of the facts. He hasn't killed anyone."

"It's true that he's not been charged with murder, but it's just a matter of time. The storm is brewing," I responded. I knew that at this point, a meeting with Drake would be pointless, even if he would agree to it.

"Write an addendum to your report, if you feel strongly about this," Drake said. "But don't include it in the report. If you attempt to include it, the judge will never see it."

"Fair enough," I said.

I wrote the report, answering the questions that Drake asked without expanding upon the facts.

In addition to a report, I added an addendum titled "Additional Information Relevant to the George Sullivan Case." In it, I laid out the additional diagnosis and its ramifications.

What happened subsequently was beyond the scope of my responsibility, and, not wishing to be sued, I was forced to leave the outcome to others.

Chapter 10
The Whitter Family

John Farmer made a visit to the Whitter home. The family lived in run down double-wide trailer, which suits their needs. *I can't believe that people live like this*, he thought to himself. *It must be barely inhabitable.*

John introduced himself to the man who answered the door. "Good morning, I'm John Farmer with Social Services."

"Who are you looking for?"

"I'm looking for Josh and Nancy Whitter," he said.

"What do you want?"

As John looked beyond the man at the room behind him, he couldn't help but notice that nothing stopped the rain from coming in and rotting the particle board floor. It already looked spongy, like it might give way when walked on. The front window was broken and covered up with cardboard and plastic sheeting that must do little to keep out the bugs in the summer or the drafty cold in the winter. The place was littered with trash, dirty clothing, and what looked like rat and dog droppings.

"I'm with social services. I came to get a safety agreement signed by you and Mrs. Whitter. Salvaging the clothing on the floor must be a real chore for you and your wife, " John said.

"Nancy hasn't been able to keep up with this mess for several years. She's been too depressed to care what the place looks like. The kids don't clean, and I don't do woman's work."

The home has become a health hazard for anyone willing to initiate efforts to clean it up, John thought. *So instead, they walk over it, around it, and through it as if it's not there.* "I'm here about a report from the school that said that one of your children, Danny Whitter, has been sexually abused by Drew Watson, the boy's uncle."

"Whoever said that is a liar," Josh said indignantly.

"Danny told Mrs. Prier, his teacher, that Drew Watson has been abusing him for years."

"This is the first I've heard such a thing. If he's lying, I'll beat the tar out of his britches."

"Calm down, Mr. Whitter, you will only make matters worse with that mindset. Is Mrs. Witter here? Can I talk to her please?"

"Sure, I'll get her for you, just a minute."

A few minutes later, a haphazard and exhausted-looking woman appeared in the doorframe.

"Hello, Mrs. Whitter. I'm John Farmer, the social worker assigned to your case," John said, extending a hand for her to shake.

"I'll feel much more at ease if you will call me Nancy."

"I take it you are the homemaker and Josh is the bread winner in this family, is that right?"

"Almost right, but neither of us is doing our duty for the family," Nancy said with a sigh. "Josh is unemployed, and I'm no better because I don't work neither."

"Well I'm sorry to her that, Nancy. Did your husband tell you why I'm here today?"

"Yes, but I don't believe it. Drew has lived with us since he was 5 years old. He's a member of the family, and we love him."

"Based on the report we received, this appears to be a very serious allegation. We can't take any chances with Drew remaining in your home," John said. "I'm going to need you and your family to come down to the office, so we can do a formal interview with Danny and the rest of your children. In the meantime, Drew is not to be in the house.

"Before I can leave today, I need you and your husband to sign this safety agreement. It is intended to protect the children from Drew. There is no doubt that Drew will have to find another place to live while the investigation is ongoing."

"I guarantee Danny's safety. He is my youngest child, my baby. He's only 10 years old. I love Drew, but he has blown my trust. I guarantee you that Drew will have no contact with my son."

"Okay, Nancy. I fear I must warn you that if you fail to protect your children, then Child Protective Services will take control, and a court order will be issued to place all of them in foster care."

"I understand, Mr. Farmer. We don't mind signing the form. We can be at your office at 9 a.m. tomorrow. I'd like to get this settled as soon as possible."

* * *

WITHIN A FEW hours of visiting the Whitter family, Nancy called John Farmer to inform him that Drew had returned to the home.

"I told him that in no uncertain terms was he to remain in the house. He and Josh ended up getting into a fight. Josh lost his cool and punched Drew. I just wanted to tell you in case he goes to the cops," Nancy said.

"Thank you, Nancy. Is Drew out of the house now?"

"Yes sir, he is. I told you, we aren't going to take any chances with Danny."

*   *   *

THE NEXT MORNING, Nancy got the family up and moving against their wishes and over their protests.

The Child Protective Services building is a large complex of offices that is buffered by a receptionist named Tatula Nelson. She monitors who goes in and who leaves.

At 9 a.m. on the dot, the Whitter family was in the building and at Tatula Nelson's desk asking for directions.

"Hello, we're here to see John Farmer," Nancy said.

Tatula scanned the appointment schedule and picked up the receiver. Her voice echoed in tandem on the overhead speaker. "Mr. Farmer, your 9 o'clock appointment is here."

Within a few moments, John arrived at the front desk to greet the family.

"Please make yourselves comfortable. The interview process will take a while, as I have to interview you all individually. I'll start with Danny. Do you have any questions?"

"No."

"Then Danny and I will go to the interview room and get down to work."

The interview room was just through a door off the lobby. It was furnished with a table, two chairs, and a tape recorder. The room was brightly illuminated by florescent lights. One wall looked like a large mirror, which turned the room into an observation deck.

John handed Danny a big teddy bear. "He is called Big Mike. Can you guess why we call him Big Mike?"

"Because he is so big," Danny said as he scooped up the bear and sat down.

"That's right, Danny," John said. "Now, do you know why we're here?"

"Am I in trouble?" Danny asked.

"No, Danny, you aren't in trouble. Why would you be in trouble?"

Danny squeezed Big Mike tightly and looked down. He was obviously struggling to fight his anxiety.

"I know this can be a scary place, Danny, but that doesn't mean you're in trouble. Sometimes the best things for us can be scary," John said, trying to reassure the boy.

"Drew told me that he would kill me if I told anyone," Danny said. "Am I going to die? Is he going to kill me?"

"When did Drew say this? Was he at your house last night?"

"Umm, for a little bit. But he and Daddy got into a fight. I was in my room, but I could hear them yelling," Danny said, his lip trembling. "Was it my fault they got into a fight? Because I told Mrs. Prier about what he did?"

"It wasn't your fault, Danny. Your parents, me, Mrs. Prier, we all want to protect you. But we can't protect you if we don't know what happened between you and Drew. Would you mind telling me?"

"I don't think it was bad. He just put his mouth on my pee pee and sucked on it hard. I thought he was going to bite it off," Danny said.

Feeling encouraged by this spontaneous disclosure, John pressured Danny for more information.

"Did he ask you to do anything with his pee pee?"

Danny considered the question for several minutes before replying. "Well, he did ask me to suck his pee pee this last time."

"How many times did he ask you to do this to him?"

Danny hesitated. "Are you going to tell Ma?"

"Danny, I promise you that nothing you tell me will get you in trouble."

"Every day when I come home from school, he wants to play the pee pee games. Sometimes I get sore from him sucking on my pee pee, and I tell him no."

"Did you see him messing with Gloria or Billy?" John asked.

"I've seen him messing with Billy, but I don't think he likes girls. I never saw him messing with Gloria."

"Well, Drew isn't supposed to talk to you anymore. If he tries to again, just tell him that you're going to tell your Da, and he will get in big trouble. Does that sound like something you can do?"

Danny nodded and looked relieved that his nightmare appeared to be almost over. They shook hands, and the three walked out of the room together, Danny, Big Mike, and John.

John Farmer next focused his attention on Billy Whitter. At 15 years old, he was a tall boy with thin, lanky arms and legs. He wore his hair in a shaggy cut similar to the style of John Lennon. His clothing was soiled, and there was a strong sour odor coming from his body that suggested he did not bathe with any regularity. He walked with the false confidence many teenagers have.

They arrived at the interview room. John entered the room first. Billy took a seat opposite of him, facing the one-way mirror.

"That's perfect," says John. "You act as if you've been here before."

Billy broke into a big smile, acting if he is part of the investigative team.

"Do you know why you are being interviewed?" John asked.

With this question, his false bravado was broken. In front of John sat a scared 15-year-old-boy.

"If this is about Danny and Drew, I don't know anything about them," he said, his voice high-pitched and too loud for the small room they were in. John noted this as unsolicited spontaneous denial.

"Who said that it had anything to do with your brother and your uncle?" John asked.

"Ma said that you think Drew has been messing with Danny," Billy said.

"I know that Drew has been messing with Danny for years. What I want to know is if Drew has messed with you," John said calmly.

"What do you take me for, a fairy?" Danny asked.

John followed his line of reasoning. "No one is suggesting that you are a homosexual. If Drew coerced you into anything, the age difference and power dynamics at play mean that it wasn't consensual."

"Well, maybe there were a couple times we messed around. But he liked to suck on my dick more than anything."

"When was the last time this happened?" John asked.

"I can't remember," Billy said.

"Do you know if Drew has done this to anyone else, maybe to Gloria?"

Billy was taken aback by the question. "I'd kill him if he messed with Gloria. She's mine!"

"You say that like you own her. Do you have a special relationship with Gloria?" John asked, suddenly suspicious of the way Billy was acting.

"Of course. She's my sister," Billy said. "I told you, I ain't a fairy. I like girls, and she's a girl."

"How long have you been having sex with Gloria?"

"A couple of years."

Feeling that there was no way they could have kept this a secret from their parents, Farmer asked, "Did your mother ever catch you having sex?"

"One time Ma walked in Gloria's room while I was riding the pony. I thought Ma would kill me, but she turned around and left before I pulled out. She never mentioned it to Gloria or me, so I guessed it was no big deal."

With this, the interview was complete, and John thanked Billy for his cooperation. Billy stopped John and asked who was on the other side of the mirror.

"My supervisor and a few people who are learning interview techniques," John said.

John's answer seemed to satisfy Billy, who seemed gratified to know that someone other than John caught the act. Billy was the first one out the door as he waved to his audience.

As he walked Billy back to his family, John had an idea. He believed that Gloria would provide more reliable information if she were interviewed by a woman. On the way to the lobby, he happened to run into Sandy Belcher, M.S.W., who was taking a break from an interview of her own.

"Hi, Sandy can I talk to you after I drop this young man off in the lobby?" he asked.

"So, you want me to do your job for you," she said, breaking into a big grin and laughing at John's expense.

"Yep! Meet me in my office in five minutes, and I'll explain what I need," John said.

After they reached the lobby, John informed the Whitter's that someone else, a woman, would be interviewing Gloria, as he wanted her to be comfortable. The family agreed, and John went back to his office.

A few minutes later, Sandy Batcher entered John's office, and he gave her a summary of the case, including everything he had just learned. Sandy was horrified to learn about the family and was more than willing to interview Gloria.

Sandy and John went to fetch Gloria from the waiting room.

"Good morning, my name is Sandy Belcher. Gloria, I'll be interviewing you and wanted to introduce myself to your family," Sandy said, shaking hands with Nancy and Josh. "Please follow me, Gloria."

The pair walked to the interview room and sat down at the table. John took a seat in the room with the one-way mirror.

Sandy began the interview by asking Gloria about school, knowing that would likely ease the anxiety.

"Do you like school, Gloria? I see that you're 14 years old, so you must be a freshman, right?

"School's okay, but it's boring," Gloria said.

"What is your favorite subject?" Sandy asked.

"I don't have a one."

"My favorite subject in school was always lunch. I could see all my friends, and we could talk about anything that was going on." Sandy responded.

Gloria cracked a small smile. "Well if I can say lunch, then that is mine too."

"Do you ever talk to your friends about your brothers?"

Looking Sandy in the eye, Gloria said, "No."

"Is there anything you want to tell me about your brothers?"

"Not really. Ma says that my uncle is messing with Danny. But I guess you already know that," she said, misinterpreting the question.

"You're correct; that is why we're here," Sandy said. "Do you know anything about this situation other than what your mother has said?"

"I've seen Drew giving Danny and Billy blow jobs."

"How many times have you seen this happen?" Sandy asked.

"Lots of times after school. Drew is always there messing with them."

"Has Drew ever messed with you?"

Gloria looked surprised and said, "No, I don't think he likes girls."

"Do your brothers like girls?" Sandy asked quietly.

Gloria paused for a moment. "Am I in trouble?" she blurted out.

"You're not in trouble, but I need you to tell the truth."

Gloria looked around the room, obviously uncomfortable, and didn't say anything for a few moments.

"I know you're nervous, but I promise you won't be in trouble for this. We all just want to keep you and your brothers safe," Sandy said, trying to reassure her.

Gloria took a deep breath and began talking incredibly fast. "Billy likes girls almost too much. He can't keep his hands off me. Whenever he starts getting handsy, he gets a hard-on and wants to have sex."

"How often does he want to have sex with you?"

"Almost every afternoon."

"Is anyone other than Billy having sex with you?"

"No! What do you take me for, a whore?" Gloria asked indignantly.

"Of course not, Gloria," Sandy said. "Are your parents aware of what Billy and you are doing?"

"I think maybe Ma has her suspicions because she caught Billy and me doing it once. But she said nothing to us. I guess she was so surprised that she had nothing to say."

"Were you afraid your mom would tell your father what you and Billy were doing?"

"I suppose so, but she wouldn't tell Dad because she knows he would kill us."

With this response recorded, the interview was over. Sandy shut off the tape recorder and brought Gloria back to her parents in the lobby.

The family sat together, not knowing what to expect. Josh Whitter didn't know if he wanted to stand up or stay seated. He stood up when he saw John, Sandy, and Gloria coming and asked if everything was alright.

"No, it's not all right. We have a big problem," John said. "I'm going to need you two to come back with me while Sandy here watches the children.

Josh looked like he was about to start screaming, but Nancy looked at her husband and gave a short shake of her head. He seemed to instantly deflate.

* * *

ANXIETY FILLED THE room, and no one talked or asked any questions. Josh and Nancy were seated on opposite sides of a round table while they waited for any news from John Farmer or Sandy Belcher.

In a separate room, the social workers were working to firm up their results and come up with a plan. After about 45 minutes, they finally entered the room in which Nancy and Josh were waiting.

"Hello again, thank you for waiting patiently and cooperating. First things first, if the kids are to be believed, and I'd rest my professional reputation on that they are, we have the worst case of incest I have encountered in my entire career."

"What do you mean?" Josh explained. "That can't be!"

"Drew Watson began sexualizing Billy when he was 5 or 6 years old, the same age he began sexually abusing Danny," John Farmer said.

This is more than Josh and Nancy could bear to hear. "Wait just a minute, are you saying that both of my boys are gay?" Josh said.

"The issue here isn't your children's sexual orientation, be they gay or straight; it's that they have been sexually molested for years by a member of your family, creating quite a bit of trauma from a young age.

"Drew appears to have made up his mind about his sexual preferences long ago, and he is a committed to being a pedophile. I consider him a danger to young boys.

"Because of the trauma they have experienced, both of your boys are capable of sexually abusing others and will have to be supervised very closely when they're around younger children."

"I'll kill them if I catch them bothering little kids," Josh said.

"That won't solve the problem," John said. "That will only result in you going to prison. Is that what you want?"

"No, that isn't what I want," Josh said, falling silent.

"We have another problem," John went on to explain. "Billy has been having sex with Gloria for several years. I know you have some knowledge of what they have been doing, Nancy, as you have caught them in the act of having sex at least once. Billy admitted this to me and then Sandy Belcher confirmed it with Gloria during her interview."

Josh looked to Nancy with a look of shock. "Why didn't you tell me about Billy and Gloria?"

"Because I was afraid you would have killed them!" Nancy shrieked.

John halted this conversation quickly. "Remember that Drew started all of this a long time ago. This is all learned behavior."

"How are they going to unlearn it?" Josh asked. "I don't want any pedophile freaks in my family."

"That is a very good question, but unfortunately, I don't know. That's what we're here to discuss. After an extensive discussion with my colleagues, we have agreed to a plan, one that will constantly be reevaluated as the needs of the children in question change.

"First, a child safety agreement is needed to protect Gloria from the sexual predation of Billy. A second safety agreement is needed to protect the boys from Drew and to protect Gloria from Danny.

"We will be working with local law enforcement to bring charges against Drew Watson for his actions against both Danny and Billy.

"We don't plan on pursuing criminal charges against Billy as an adult, as there is ample evidence that he was abused for years from Drew Watson. Instead, he will be placed at NOVA Group Home for the foreseeable future. This is to protect both Gloria and Billy.

"Danny and Gloria can both remain in your care, as there is no evidence of these two acting out sexually with one another.

"We are also making it mandatory that the entire family, especially the three children, see a psychologist. The specialist who came to our minds first was Dr. Trattoria. He specializes in children who have been sexually abused. Dr. Trattoria will teach all of you how to manage your anger and to help the children understand and process the trauma that they've experienced," John concluded.

*   *   *

A FEW DAYS after Billy was placed in NOVA Group Home, it was time for my assessment of the oldest Whitter child. I had been given a detailed case history of the entire Whitter family from the case manager, which I used to construct a summary of events for my own reference.

I drove to Kinston to see my client. The outside of the group home complex looked like a prison compound with six-foot fences topped with razor wire. The only things missing were watch towers with armed guards.

There was a remote keypad that allowed me to me to talk to a guard inside the building. After presenting my credentials and passing the screening test, I was admitted. Within minutes, I was walking into the compound's front office, where I was directed to the building that housed Billy.

I walked to the door and knocked. An older man opened the door, a man by the name of Charles Lott. Charles and his wife, Linda, were new to NOVA Group Home, so I'd done my research prior to my visit.

Charles and Linda Lott were in their late 50s. Charles was a retired programmer for John Deer Inc., a career that was a far cry from what he was doing now.

According to Charles, he became a group home parent as a way to give back for all the good fortune he has had in his life. Neither he nor Linda had any experience with emotionally disturbed and abused teens, so they had no idea what they were getting into. I was almost as interested to see how they were handling their new life as I was to meet with my client.

"Good morning, I'm Dr. Trattoria. I am here for a conference with the group home parents."

The group home parents had plenty to tell me about Billy.

"Since he arrived here, he has been in three fights and is constantly challenging our authority. We've had to keep him on Level III since his arrival, and now we have him on escape precautions," Linda said.

"What has him so paranoid?" Charles asked. "He reacts badly to everyone. I don't know how long we can safely house him here. Most of the boys talk of wanting to kill him."

Trattoria sighed. "Do your best. I'll look into a placement at Butner Psychiatric Hospital. They may be better equipped to handle him. When can I see him?"

"You can see him now, but he is dressed in his skivvies," Linda says. "Do you want him in his street clothing?"

"No, not if he hasn't earned the right to wear them."

Dressed in a robe and his underwear, the boy was waiting in his room for me to arrive. I followed Linda and Charlie Lott into the room.

"What does he want? He looks like a shrink to me," Billy asked after giving me a once over.

"What gave me away?" I asked.

"I don't know. Maybe it has something to do with the brief case you are carrying."

"Very observant, Billy, but something else had to cue you to my identity. What was it?"

"You aren't dressed like a janitor, and you don't look like a cop, so I guessed you was a shrink."

"You're right. I just need some of your time and patience. I'm Dr. Trattoria, and I'm here to give you some tests. Is that okay with you?"

"I've got lots of time to give, but I'm short on patience."

"So, tell me what a nice kid like you is doing in a place like this?" I asked. I already knew why he was here, but I had found that it's better to let patients explain rather than go in acting as though I know everything about them already.

"It all started with a social worker who thought I'd keep nailing my sister," Billy said with a roll if his eyes.

"Was he right?" I asked. "Would you have continued to 'nail' your sister, as you worded it, if you were still at home?"

"I guess so. But only because she wanted it."

"And I guess since you're her sex slave, you didn't have a choice?" I asked rhetorically.

Billy couldn't help but grin. "You're the only one who got it right. She's a nympho, and I can't satisfy her."

"Enough jokes for now, Billy. Let's get the testing out the way, so that we can have time to really talk.

"We will start with drawing these nine cards. Do the best you can."

Billy put forth a good effort in the testing and proved to be cooperative. The first test was an intelligence test that was intended to rule out retardation and to gauge his neurological integrity.

Billy tested with average intelligence and showed no sign of neurological disorders. He is not a genius, by any means, but he has average IQ of 105.

I assessed Billy for character disorder using a Rorschach test, which cannot be faked by anyone who hasn't studied it in detail. There was no doubt that pathology was present given his history of acting out sexually with his younger sister. Billy tested positive for self-aggrandizing in both fantasy and behavior. He believes that he is special and that he can only be understood and appreciated by someone like himself.

An excessive need for admiration, as well as a sense of entitlement, was also strongly indicated. No remorse was evident, which strongly suggested a narcissistic personally disorder. Neither depression nor thought disorder was noted in the results.

His paranoia scales were pathological, and they are not just a reaction to the current predicament. Billy saw links between remote elements that were not there. He made comments like, "There are eyes staring at me following my movements." His response was visceral, and he complained that the cards had a demonic quality.

His anger was ubiquitous, and his self-righteousness was typical of someone who feels persecuted. At the end of the day, he blamed the social worker, John Farmer, for the loss of his sexual partner and for his incarceration. At the time of the test, Billy did not exhibit the slightest awareness of what he had done to his sister or that it was wrong.

The Greek philosopher Epictetus had some insight into Billy's dilemma. He said, "Men are not disturbed by events that surround them, but by the view they take of them."

According to his Uncle Drew, it was normal to have sex with your brother and sister, so in Billy's mind, he is being persecuted by the system for acting normal.

When the testing was completed, Billy was exhausted. I packed up my testing materials, said goodbye to Mr. and Mrs. Lott, and headed for my Miata. Within 35 minutes, I was home, putting my house key in the lock of the front door.

In my view, Billy, Danny, and Gloria were raised in such a hostile environment that they did not know right from wrong. Billy had no moral grounds for judging right and wrong where sexual relations with his sister are concerned.

There was no right or wrong when they began experimenting with sex as children. Sex was a coping mechanism that allowed them to feel loved. Their living conditions were so extreme that the value used to gauge the quality of life was ephemeral. Billy interpreted the gentleness and kindness that Gloria showed him as love.

Billy will spend six months at NOVA Group Home before returning home to the family, which is undergoing a change for the better. Gloria is learning to say no to the advances of others, including Billy, and learning to respect herself.

Danny remains confused about his sexual identity but still has time to learn. All three children will continue to go to therapy. Drew Watson was sent to prison after a short trial and lost his way, choosing sexual perversion over therapy and healing.

Chapter 11
One and One Makes Three

First thing Monday morning, the office phone started ringing.

"Good morning, you've reached Dr. Trattoria's office. This is Sophie speaking, how may I help you?"

"Good morning, this is Nancy Gray, the Director of Nursing Services at Silver Springs Nursing Home. I'm requesting a consultation. Does Dr. Trattoria have a hole in his schedule?"

"Hi, Nancy, of course he does. How soon do you need the consult done?"

"We would like her seen this week, if possible. The patient's name is Martha Story. She is a psychiatric patient who was involuntarily committed to the facility two years ago. Martha is in need of a competency assessment that was overlooked in a rush to get her into our facility. To say that it is overdue would be minimizing the issue. The original psychiatric diagnosis ought to be set aside until the test can be done. Martha was traumatized by events at the time, and she has spent two years in here getting herself together."

"We would be happy to take the case, provided she agrees to pay for the competency assessment," Sophie said.

"She has money and can afford the co-pay. The fly in the ointment is her sister-in-law, JoAnne Story. She has healthcare power of attorney. Up to this point, she has had some objections to Martha leaving the nursing home and recovering her independence, but I think the results of Dr. Trattoria's assessment might change her mind."

"What has been her objection up to now?" Sophie asked.

"I believe she was afraid that Martha would be taken advantage of by unscrupulous people and lose her inheritance."

"If you have a few moments, I will connect you with Dr. Trattoria. I think it would be beneficial for him to get some background information on the case from you prior to his assessment."

"Of course, I would be happy to speak with him," Nancy said.

"Please hold while I connect you."

* * *

"GOOD MORNING, THIS is Dr. Trattoria," I said. "I understand that you have a patient in need of a competency examination. Sophie has also told me that there are some issues with relatives, is that correct?"

"Yes, Dr. Trattoria, that's exactly right."

"Is there an accounting procedure to ensure that her assets are protected?"

"I can ask, but I don't think so."

"That sounds like one plus one makes three. JoAnne has figured out how to get control of Martha's assets but for one tiny detail: how to convince Martha to go along with the plan," I said. "It sounds like Martha Story wants her life back, including her financial independence. Her sister-in-law has executive power and wants to keep it, along with her resources."

"I can't figure out why JoAnne is worried about her sister-in-law gaining control of her resources unless there are accounting irregularities," Nancy said.

"That just could have something to do with it," I responded. "Can you open an inquiry with the bank on Martha's behalf? Getting an accounting will be quick and easy. It seems like a fait accompli with JoAnne Story managing the finances and paying the bills."

"Sure," Nancy responded. "But what about the fact that Martha was declared incompetent by the court? How do we reverse that?"

"To get the court to reverse that decision will require a second court order, and that will take a lawyer. Why did the court take away her right to manage her resources?"

"Ostensibly it was because she had wasted her inheritance and was derelict in how she spent her money," Nancy said.

"All right, I know an attorney who will probably take the case. His name is Stuart Jones."

We made plans for an appointment on Thursday afternoon. I also offered to call the attorney to see if he could be persuaded to accept the case pro bono. That problem was on its way to being solved.

*   *   *

AT ABOUT 1:15 p.m. on Thursday afternoon, I arrived at the nursing home. I asked to see Nancy Gray and to see Martha's chart.

Nancy acted as the patient advocate and provided the history as best she could recall it. "She has had no visitors for months. No one has taken her out on passes or visited her over the holidays. She had no visitors on her birthday, which was February 18th."

No explanation was given for the neglect. It is what it is.

I met Martha Story in the dining room of the nursing home. It was all but empty except for two cafeteria workers arranging chairs and tables. The workers were focused on their task and conversation and showed no interest in our conversation.

Martha Story was a woman of above average height, especially given her age. She wore clothing that camouflaged her corpulence and allowed her to slouch when she walked. Her gray hair was streaked yellow, a result of her chain smoking. Her voice was raspy due to her smoking and the start of emphysema.

"So, what did you do to get yourself into a place like this?" I asked somewhat playfully.

Martha has a difficult time making eye contact. "I don't know you. I have never met you, so why should I tell you what happened?"

"I'm here often seeing patients, so I presumed that you recognized me. I'm Dr. Trattoria. And I'm here to do a competence assessment of you."

"Haven't you familiarized yourself with my chart?" she asked.

"I took a look, but your chart is like an encyclopedia," I said. "It will take hours to review what has been written. Plus, I'd like to hear about it from you. It's my personal belief that you can't believe everything written in these charts. It's going to take a conversation with you before I can form an opinion about you."

I'm a little-old fashioned. I look for an opportunity to get to know my patients firsthand. Taking my time to get to know the patient is more labor-intensive, but in the long run, the payoff is worth the investment.

"So why don't we get started?" I asked.

Martha nodded she agreement, and I opened my notebook.

"Just for the record, please state your full name."

"My full name is Martha Sue Ward Story," she said with all the confidence she could muster.

"And what is your full address."

"I lost my home when I had to file for bankruptcy," Martha said a little wistfully. "My sister-in-law refused to release my savings account and took over my social security account. I was broke. But I am sorry, I didn't answer your question. My only address is Silver Spring Nursing Home, 135 Adam Creek Road, Room 225, New Bern, North Carolina. Do you need my zip too?"

"That won't be necessary, Ms. Story. Will you tell me your age and birthday and where were you born, please."

"Can I trust you to be discrete and not to publish nor write it on the wall of a public restroom?" She asked with a glint of sarcasm in her voice.

I smiled and assured her that my lips were sealed on that matter.

"You can count on me to keep your secret. Anything you tell me is confidential. I am bound to secrecy unless I am court-ordered to reveal by a judge."

"Well alright then, my birthday is April 21, 1925, and I was born in Hackensack, New Jersey,"

"Can you tell me the name of the 44th president of the United States?"

"Are you kidding me? Can you give me a hint?" she asked innocently.

"No hint," I responded. "Although the president before him was a Bush. That should provide you with some helpful information."

"Oh, I know," she said. "That African-American guy, Barack Obama. Am I right?"

"That's right! Now let's begin your evaluation."

"Oh, I thought that your questions were the evaluation," she said, obviously hoping that the ordeal was over.

"I have a feeling that you will do very well on the tests," I said trying to reassure her. "Let's start with some drawing tests."

I brought out the Bender Visual-Motor Gestalt test and handed her the first card. She looked at card and then drew the geometric pattern from memory rather than just copying it. The next eight were handled much the same way.

"Am I doing okay, Doctor?" she asked, needing reassurance.

"You're doing fine, Martha."

The Wechsler Adult Intelligence Scale (WAIS) takes about an hour to administer and leaves most people drained. The picture completion test is a test that measures the ability to form a completed image. With one or more elements left out, the patient has to fill in the missing parts. Martha whipped through the test, restoring her self-confidence. By the time we reached the arithmetic test, she was beaming with pride.

"That was a snap," she said. The vocabulary test was below her functional vocabulary, and she breezed through it without a hitch. When it was done, her full-scale IQ was 115, a full standard deviation above the mean.

There was no evidence of disorder in her behavior, but to furnish a complete assessment, a Rorschach had to be administrated. The test showed freedom from distortion and flexibility in reason. No evidence of thought disorder was noted. Her results supported freedom from dementia, which was also demonstrated on the WAIS.

"I appreciate you taking time to show that I'm okay, that I can be trusted to manage my own affairs," Martha said with a large smile. "I guess I placed my trust in the wrong people. I thought my financial advisor, Michael Jacobs, would the one person I could trust with my money. I never thought he would steal it.

"But he did, and then he took off after he cleaned out my account, thinking he got it all. Efforts to locate him have been futile, but the state attorney was angry.

"I also filed a complaint with the district attorney, who issued an order to have him arrested if he comes back into the county. He is not likely to come back here, knowing that he is a wanted man. I know who has control of my money now, my brother and sister-in-law."

"I don't want history repeated itself. I will ask your attorney to file a petition with the court to have your family removed as financial guardians. That should return the power over your finances back to you."

After the competency assessment was finished, I thanked her for cooperating and told her that she would have the results within a week's time.

Nancy was one of the first to hear from the court decision. Martha was given her freedom from the nursing home. Her inheritance and monthly income were returned to her, giving her plenty of money to support herself.

Cases like Martha's are all too frequent but are seldom investigated. The greater the social status of the family, the more difficult it is to point fingers and to prove the case.

Chapter 12
Oh, When the Saints Come Marching In

R ichard Johnson was referred to me by his oncologist, Dr. Patrick Gregory. After his initial visit, it was over a month before Richard returned. He said it was critical that he see me on that day.

At 3 o'clock that afternoon, he arrived at my office and told me what a difficult time he was having accepting Dr. Gregory's diagnosis. His findings were based on evidence from CAT scans, symptomatic pain, and blood tests.

He had insisted on a second opinion before he would to talk to Dr. Gregory about his prognosis, which was dire. According to Dr. Gregory, he was dying from a particularly virulent form of cancer. There was little that medicine could do to slow the progression of his disease. This denial is why he had missed his previous appointments.

Richard Johnson was above average height when he stood erect, a feat that was impossible for him much of the time due to the pain in his abdomen. Due to weeks of chemotherapy and radiation, he had lost most of his hair and was sick to his stomach. To get even with his treatment, he had shaved the rest of head. His clothing hung on him like he was a clothing rack and appeared three sizes too big. There was three-day growth of stubble on his cheeks and chin. His eyes had large, dark circles around them, a testimony to sleepless nights. There was no question that the spirit keeping him alive was fading quickly.

"What's wrong with me?" Richard asked. "I know I have cancer, but why do I have to be angry all the time? Even when I am not down in the dumps, there is no joy. There are always tests, treatments, and the drudgery of living day after day. Even getting out of bed is a chore because I never feel well enough to do anything. Old habits are difficult to overcome, so I still go to work. Even so, I get no pleasure out of it.

"Most of my time is spent sitting staring at the papers in front of me. I don't think I can handle this much longer," he said, his voice cracking.

Before I could respond, I caught sight of the .38 caliber gun laying cloaked in his lap. "What are your plans for the gun?" I asked.

"I thought I could make up my mind about what to do with it after talking to you."

"Can you trust me to hold it for you?" I asked.

"No, not really. I have to keep it right where it is, till I have decided what I'm going to do."

"This makes me nervous."

"I'm not nervous," Richard said. "But I've got to find something that makes the pain stop. So far prayers haven't helped. My relationship with God is torn like the Shroud of Turin. I can't forgive Him for abandoning me. Religion and faith have lost all meaning."

"When I was diagnosed with cancer, no one from the church called to find out what happened to the 9 a.m. cantor. I sang in the choir for four years, liturgical season after liturgical season. I never got a single call from the choir director or any of the choir members. I don't consider myself special, but a call from someone would have been appreciated. That was the thanks I got for all my practice and my devotion to making Mass meaningful.

"I can't eat any solid food because the thought of eating makes me nauseous. When I'm able to get food past my lips, I throw up. My pain is unbearable. The only relief I get is when I'm able to sleep for about two hours with the aid of oxycodone, and that shit makes me sick to my stomach, too. I want to die. I guess if the cancer doesn't kill me, the doctors will with all this radiation and chemo. I have three more weeks of chemotherapy before they stop to measure the size of the tumors."

"Are you working with hospice?" I asked.

"Yeah, I see Brian Brown with the hospice team twice a week. We pray a lot to accept the will of God, but that is a sure thing. It's accepting the inevitable. Is this all there is to my life? There is no point in continuing the pain and suffering when I can end it now."

"That depends upon your religious principals and beliefs," I said.

"What difference is there between the doctor killing me with radiation or ending it now with one squeeze of a trigger? I'll skip the radiation."

With that, he raised the gun to his mouth and fired once, driving his head back and covering the office wall with blood and brains.

Horrified, I grabbed the phone and dialed 9-1-1. I was traumatized by the event, but I was sure that Richard is dead.

It took less than 10 minutes for the detectives to arrive and secure the office, but the body of Richard Johnson remained where he had been sitting for another hour while I spoke to the detectives, and they examined the crime scene. His body fluids seeped into the seat and onto the floor. The odor of death was overwhelming and made breathing difficult.

When they removed the body for the morgue, I was relieved. With time to think, I decided to call his parish priest.

Getting Father Tully on the line was apparently as difficult as reaching Dr. Moeller. When I agreed to talk to the parish secretary, I was told that the priest was out, and I'd have to wait for Father Tully to return and collect his messages.

Around 8 p.m. that night, Father Tully finally called me back.

"I thought you had banker's hours," I said. "I wouldn't trade hours with you for all the tea in China."

"Unfortunately, I do not," Father Tully said. "How are you doing, Tony?"

"I'm okay, just exhausted. Did you hear the news about Richard Johnson? He killed himself this afternoon."

"What happened?" Father Tully asked, the shock evident in his voice.

I explained the details to Father Tully, all the blood and gore included.

"You mean he killed himself right there in your office?" he said. "Wow, that must have been tough to witness. How can I help?"

"I'm still shook up, but my nerves are beginning to settle down. The medical examiner collected Richard two hours ago, and that helped.

I feel like I need some Jack Daniels to calm my nerves."

"Would you and 'Jack' like some company? I can be there in less than 10 minutes."

"I'd love your company, Father, but I've got to get home. I have to ask you, did Richard mention killing himself to you?"

"No. I knew he was depressed, but he never mentioned suicide. He kept his thoughts to himself."

"Well, it's been a hell of a day. I need to go home and clear my mind with a view of nature, a glass of wine, and my beautiful wife."

"See you later, Tony," Father Tully said.

When a tragedy happens in the office or in my personal life, it has to be processed. Was there something I should have done to avert it?

Richard Johnson was a patient who I cared for, but there was nothing I could have done to prevent his suicide.

He wanted to end his life, and I was not made aware of his decision until moments before he carried it out. The decision to kill himself was one between him and his maker. He didn't seek my approval to commit suicide and wasn't looking to be talked out of killing himself. He was active in hospice for months before reaching the decision. After reaching the decision, he was at peace.

Richard no longer blamed God for his cancer. There was no animosity toward the church, and no sense of abandonment by the people in the church. He accepted that bad things happened to good people. His cancer was a part of his living. Dying is a consequence of living. He did not have a choice in dying, just when he would die. He coped with the cancer as long as his body would allow. He said his goodbyes and ended it.

When my time comes, I hope that I have the courage that Richard displayed.

Chapter 13
Clay County Department of Social Services

"Hi, Dr. Trattoria, this is Heather Roach from Clay County Department of Social Services. I'm calling to see if you have time in your schedule to take a court-ordered custody case."

"How quickly do you need me?" I asked.

"How about yesterday?" Heather said with a laugh.

"I can squeeze you in tomorrow morning. How does 10 a.m. sound?"

"We can be there," Heather said.

"Great. I will have my office manager send over an intake evaluation form. Please fill it out ahead of time, just so I have the basics of the case. In the meantime, what can you tell me about the family?"

"The father's name is Dennis Buck, and the mother's name is Connie Fowl. The child's name is Donald Buck. The purpose of the evaluation is to address some parenting issues. Each parent has to be evaluated for fitness to parent. We need to know which parent is best suited to raise the child.

"We will need you to complete a full range of psychological tests on both of the respondents and the child. Each parent needs to be interviewed separately."

"Has the child been interviewed in the past with respect to the parenting question?" I asked.

"Yes. A child psychologist in Tennessee, a Dr. Brian Smith with the Moslem Counseling Services, was the first to interview him. Dr. Jessie James, another child psychologist, has also worked with the child and his father for the past two years."

"Just the child and the father?"

"That is correct. Until a few weeks ago, the child had had no contact of any kind with his mother for two years. The prohibition was enforced by his father and his therapist."

"Thank you, this has been informative. I'll need transcripts of the boy's exams and any reports from his family psychologist and teachers. I look forward to seeing you tomorrow morning."

After hanging up with Heather, I spent quite a bit of time reviewing the background of the case. This had been quite the custody battle.

A paternity suit was filed, and the investigator found that Dennis was the father of the child. Dennis announced his intent to fight for full custody of Donald. There was a mutual exchange of accusations of neglect and abuse, but the most damaging accusations were made by Dennis. He claimed that Connie was neglectful of Donald and that, as a result, he was small for his age. He also claimed that Donald could not feed himself and that he still used a pacifier to comfort himself as he went to sleep, well past the age when it would be normal.

As fighting for custody hit a fever-pitch, Connie's functioning declined. She stopped cooking and cleaning, and she started drinking and smoking pot. Fear of losing her son became her sole obsession. Connie was convinced by Dennis' bravado that he would not allow her to have any contact with Donald.

Her social and financial instability raised her fears that he would make good on his promise. Dennis's criminal history did little to reassure her that she could even win visitation, let alone full custody. Dennis was gifted in his ability to intimidate others. All efforts to reassure Connie failed, and her fear of Dennis grew as time passed.

Dennis was eventually granted sole custody of Donald. Three years later, Connie finally got an attorney to help her fight for her share of custody.

* * *

THE NEXT MORNING, I met with Heather. She revealed that since meeting with his mother, Donald had begun wetting himself daily.

"We don't know for sure if this is a coincidence or if the bed-wetting is related to the visit with his mother," Heather explained. "Dr. Smith reached the conclusion that the mother's visit triggered the recall of past trauma."

"The notes from his last session may shed some light on the issue," I said. "Let's see what Dr. Smith has to say: 'Donald had a nightmare of his father, who was very angry. He had a difficult time putting the memory into words. It seemed the juxtaposition of the memory and the feeling was more than a coincidence.' It seems to me that the father's wrath was burned into the memory of the 6-year old. Why was the boy so frightened of his father?"

"That's a great question, Dr. Trattoria. I hope you can help us answer it," Heather said. "After the mother's visit, Dennis began complaining about some alleged sexual aggression from Donald. Dennis wanted to link the two incidences together, but neither his classroom teachers nor his principal had observed any kind of sexual behavior from Donald and reported that Donald was an exemplary student."

"Are you implying that Dennis was making these stories up?" I asked.

"That's an alternative interpretation we are considering. But the question is why he would want to make his son look like a sexual deviant," Heather responded.

"When I read Dr. James' report, he appeared to have accepted the reports from Dennis at face value. His conclusion was that Donald posed a threat to other students. Dr. James does not document anger except for what Dennis reported. The social worker who relied on his therapist for factual information never verified what Dennis reported. The nurse practitioner assigned to the case also relied on the therapist's report to generate his own opinion and didn't verify what was said.

"I believe that all the forensic evaluations appear to have been plagiarized. This reminds me of that children's song, 'All around the mulberry bush, the monkey chased the weasel.' You know the next two verses. Nobody verified what Dennis said, and all of them accepted the reports as factual. It appears that Dennis succeeded in manipulating Donald's therapist, the social workers, the sexual abuse investigators, the forensic psychologist, and the courts. He has created his own version of reality."

"That's what we believe. We just need your help to prove it," Heather said.

"Of course," I said. "I'll need to interview both parents and test both of them. But the most important question we need to answer is what all of this will mean to Donald's future. The behaviors that Donald's father described could have been the result of being unfairly treated by his father and others. A kid gets even with adults who treat him unfairly in his own way. Donald's behaviors transformed into predictable rage and physical aggression directed at himself. He reportedly took a poop in the tub and smeared it all over himself and the walls. Have you heard of anyone smearing feces on themselves?" I asked Heather.

"I have never heard of someone doing this to themselves. And yet no one questioned him about the incident. This was an aggressive and violent behavioral reaction to something. The question is, what triggered this response?"

"There are many ways that a child can express his anger. Self-injury is the most frequent form. The most common types include burning and biting themselves. What gave Donald the idea to smear poop on himself? It is possible that he believes the things said about him are true. If you are told that you did something often enough, you question whether or not, it happened."

*   *   *

THE DAY OF my interview with Dennis Buck arrived.

"Good morning, Mr. Buck," I said as he came through the door of my office. "Please take a seat."

Dennis was a short man. He was 5 feet and 5 inches tall, but what he lacked in height, he made up for with an inflated opinion of himself. He was dressed in casual clothing that was soiled with body fluids and the pungent smell of tobacco.

His hair was thinning, and he had a friar's cap on the back of his head. His face had a beard that gave him a gremlin appearance, and he carried himself as if he were Tom Selleck walking across a movie set.

"Good morning, Doctor. What did you say your name was?"

"I did not say, but it's Dr. Trattoria," I responded.

"Is that Spanish?"

"No, it's Italian."

"I could have sworn it was Spanish or Portuguese," he persisted.

"My name is derived from trattorias, which means hospitality as it is spoken in Sicily."

"So that would make you a Sicilian!" he said, as if he earned a prize for guessing my ethnic identity.

"That's right, and you're here for a court assessment to evaluate your suitability to parent your son, Donald. It's my understanding that you had a long-standing positive relationship with Dr. James. Do you have a different opinion?" I asked.

"It was all positive. Donald seemed to enjoy our visits," Dennis said. He sat up tall, believing he was scoring points.

It was important for me to understand Dennis' childhood if I was to understand who he was now. I started prodding him about childhood memories and experiences.

"I did not like school, and I got failing grades throughout elementary school," Dennis said. "My problem with failing grades ended when I entered middle school. After I achieved success in middle school, I quit school entirely. Living with Pop was a real challenge. His temper was like quicksilver, and you never knew when he would explode. When he went off, no one was safe. When Mom left him without telling me, I did not know what to do. I continued living with him. Somehow, things settled down. My father was a sail maker, and I learned the trade of making sails from him. I worked for 10 years under his tutorage and started working in his business with him. When his business failed, I was obviously out of a job.

"I learned to play the guitar and to sing. I wasn't such a great singer, but I was capable of carrying a tune. I figured if Willie Nelson could do it, anyone could. Besides, I wasn't interested in the Grand Ole Opry, just in earning enough to survive. I loved being the center of attention. I am resourceful and persevering. Most of my problems would be solved if I could find a woman who would support me in a style that suited my needs, but unfortunately, the women I am attracted to need a handout," Dennis said with a sigh.

With his background collected, I began his psychological test. The first test up was an IQ test. Dennis achieved an average score, somewhere between the 93rd and 106th percentile. He was no genius, but he was resourceful. What he lacked in intellect, he made up in cunning.

I next administered an achievement test. Like his IQ test results, his test scores were all in the average range. No discrepancies between achievement and aptitude were recorded. The noteworthy differences between his test results and the problems he had in the classroom had to be due to other dynamics.

The results from the achievement supported the notion that he could read and answer the questions of the Minnesota Multiphasic Personality Inventory (MMPI). The conclusion was that the test was valid and reliable. Dennis attempted to shape the outcome of the test. He answered the questions in an effort to make himself look better. He denied questions that might have made him look bad. He tried to shape the appearance as if he were a social conformist and avoided any evidence of pathology. He denied problems with hostility, suspicion, family dissention, and a lack of confidence. His superlative scores were elevated, suggesting narcissism.

Dennis had a two-point code configuration. Psychiatric patients with similar codes often have somatic symptom disorders, and some have dissociative disorders. These code types tend to be rather immature, egocentric, selfish, and histrionic. Although outgoing and socially motivated, their relationships are shallow and superficial.

Even after only spending a short time with Dennis, those results seemed to be accurate.

After I finished up with Dennis, I needed to meet and evaluate Connie. When Connie arrived for her appointment, she had the appearance of someone who was scared to death. She was about 6 feet tall, and her uncombed hair made her even taller. She weighed nearly 300 pounds and wore a dress that covered her like a tent. Connie walked with a lumbering flat-footed gait that made her appear as if she was ready to topple over. She spoke in an articulate and polished manner. If you listened to her speech without seeing her, you would never connect the dots.

"I was born in Texas and raised in Kentucky by my mother, Rosie Donavan," Connie began. "My mother had four children, and I am the oldest. She worked in convenience stores and with an income tax group during tax season. She had a history of alcohol abuse, which ran in my family, starting with my maternal grandfather, Robert Donavan. He died of hepatic alcohol complications. He was found guilty of having sexually abused his children and was sent to prison. My mother was married three times, and each one of her husbands was more unstable than the last. My father was unemployed and barely in the picture.

"I did not know who to trust, probably due to the fact that I had a history of being sexually abused by my female babysitter. I reported the assault to a school counselor when I was 13 years old.

"I liked school and earned average grades. I quit school when I was sixteen because things were chaotic. I married my first husband at the age of 17 and left him three months later after a fight resulted in a broken nose and two missing teeth. I had no children from that marriage and moved back to North Carolina to live with my mother. I met Dennis at a bar he was singing in, and we had a child, Donald. I remained with him for three years, supporting myself and my son."

"Speaking of your ex-husband and your son, Dennis has made some serious allegations about you in relation to your son. How do those allegations make you feel?"

"I don't understand them. I am modest and never bathed or used the toilet without closing the door. I taught Donald boundaries and modesty from the time he was a toddler. If he walked in on me while I was dressing, I would correct him. He slept in his own bed after six months, but occasionally he would sneak into my bed in the early morning to snuggle.

"He loved bath time. As his mother, I bathed Donald in a tub until he was six, cleaning his genitals in the tub while bathing him. This was the only time I touched his penis. I never saw Donald masturbate. I was asked about the allegations made by Dennis, that I let Donald blow bubbles on my nipples, and I was appalled."

The results from her IQ test indicated that she was functioning in the average range of intelligence. Her achievement scores were average and consistent with her reports in school. According to Connie, her report card was average, and she never had discipline issues with her teachers.

Connie was given the MMPI as a means of collecting her personality. She had a two-point configuration of 67/76. Graham's third edition had no comparable two-point code. The interpretation of high-point scores were not correlated with known patterns of pathology. Her moderate elevations on these two scales says nothing definitive. Connie had no evidence of psychopathology. Her profile indicated that she was capable of supporting her son. Obsessive-compulsive and ritualistic behavior were exposed. These feelings often center on feelings of insecurity and inferiority.

Connie presented herself as a much more integrated personality than her test results suggest. She was not free to discuss her mistakes in dealing with the men in her life. Her profile suggests that she is a target for aggressive males. Connie's neediness makes her a willing victim if her companion shows any display of validation or approval. Her low self-esteem and difficulty with decisions make parenting her son a problem.

Connie reported that she had a history of alcohol abuse that resulted from her fear of being alone. It is also likely that she resorted to alcohol abuse in order to self-medicate her anxiety and depression.

This was going to be a difficult situation to resolve. It seemed that Donald became the prize Dennis was searching for. It was Donald who was capable of meeting his father's needs instead of the other way around. It was a little 6-year-old boy who symbolized security by providing a paycheck. It was the perfect solution for Dennis, so he would never have to work again.

The results from my evaluation supported Connie's claim of being the more qualified parent. In spite of the problems with alcohol and drugs, she was less frightening than Dennis. The discrepancies between the teacher's reports of Donald's behavior and Dennis' reports of his predatory behavior were more than noteworthy. Dennis appeared obsessed with accusing his son of sexual transgressions. He raised concerns about his own sexual integrity, but no reports were filed concerning Dennis' sexual misconduct.

Conclusion
Taking a Break for Now

As a psychologist, I was constantly caught between the flood of patients seeking my services and the rising costs of working in the modern healthcare system.

There is a renaissance of new solutions to age-old problems. I don't feel like changing what I've been doing successfully because an actuary for an insurance company says that I must. I have been in the business of finding solutions to problems for 40 years, but that doesn't mean someone can't build a better mouse trap or find a solution that works as well.

Considering the ebb and flow of the mental health reformation, I have been clinging to the plank that has kept me afloat a long time. But the challenge of justifying everything that I say is not worth it. My heart is no longer in this contest.

For 40 years, I have put others needs ahead my own needs.

The needs of my patients are always with me. I don't stand a chance of getting my own needs served if I don't take a stance in my own defense. Insight is a developmental process for the therapist, as well as the patient. My time has come. Reality has struck a chord, and I'm listening to the tune it's playing.

My time is running out. I've collected my universal truths, and I have worked through their obscurity. I have discovered which truths work for me. Time is a commodity that we can't manufacture for ourselves. I'm left with my faith. If there are universal truths beyond the Nicene Creed, I haven't discovered them.

www.ingramcontent.com/pod-product-compliance
Lightning Source LLC
Chambersburg PA
CBHW070925270326
41927CB00011B/2728